RELATIONS AMONG RELIGIONS TODAY

RELATIONS AMONG RELIGIONS TODAY

A HANDBOOK OF
POLICIES AND PRINCIPLES

EDITED BY

MOSES JUNG
SWAMI NIKHILANANDA
HERBERT W. SCHNEIDER

LEIDEN
E. J. BRILL
1963

PRINTED IN THE NETHERLANDS

TABLE OF CONTENTS

PART ONE

OFFICIAL FORMULATIONS OF NORMS BY CHRISTIAN RELIGIOUS BODIES

PART TWO

STATEMENTS BY REPRESENTATIVES OF RELIGIOUS BODIES CONCERNING THE PRINCIPLES AND POLICIES GOVERNING RELATIONS WITH OTHER RELIGIONS

PART THREE

ESSAYS ON GENERAL PRINCIPLES

APPENDIX

DIRECTORY OF INTERNATIONAL ORGANIZATIONS CONCERNED WITH INTER-RELIGIOUS RELATIONS

PREFACE

It is commonly supposed by distant observers that religions are and must be rivals: being alternative ways to deliverance from evil, they are taken to be competitors for the souls of men, and hence naturally inclined to be suspicious, disdainful, jealous, if not resentful toward each other. And by the faithful, too, it is often supposed that anyone who is devoted whole-heartedly to a single family, country, cause, or Savior is unable to appreciate or respect a like loyalty in others to other faiths. The life of faith precludes a positive inter-faith attitude, they say, for not only is any faith superior to an inter-faith attitude of liberal disinterest, but it is in the nature of love and faith to be discriminating and partial. However, any one who knows the facts of inter-religious relations knows that they have changed radically in the course of history and that notable changes in attitudes are taking place now. This is true both for organized religious bodies in their policies toward each other and for religious individuals in their sentiments toward persons of other faiths. Complicating the state of religious affairs still more is the (ancient and reputable) belief, that above or beneath all particular religions there is among men a natural or universal respect for religion as such and that consequently there is a natural ground of reasonable tolerance in any genuine religion for what is common or universal to all. In other words, any God that is worshipped is believed to be more than just *a* god among others, and any Savior that is trusted is believed to be truly divine in some universal sense.

In view of such diversified opinions about how religions regard each other or should regard each other, there is a persistent demand among theoretical students of religion as well as among practical believers to know what relations actually obtain today among members of different faiths and how religious bodies actually formulate whatever inter-religious policies and principles they may have. To investigate such facts among religious individuals would carry the investigator into an enormous sociological analysis of current religious behavior, feeling, and belief. The facts of mixed marriages, of the religious regulation of caste or racial segregations, the limits of tolerance, the spread of inter-religious cooperative benevolences, etc. are among the most complicated facts about which sociologists, psychologists and moralists venture generalizations. This is an important vast area in the general field of morals, tastes, and norms. But there are two more limited factual questions which may be investigated more readily: (1). What are the norms which religious bodies are actually formulating for their members in their relations with members of other religions *in matters of faith and worship*?; (2). What kind of criticism and rationalization are these norms receiving in current discussions among leaders of the chief religions in the world today? It is to these two questions that this handbook is devoted. In other words, quite apart from the many moral, political and esthetic problems which are generated when members of different faiths get together, there are *problems of faith or cultus* which are central to the attempts on the part of the different religions to explain themselves to each other and to justify their sympathy or lack of sympathy with other ways of worshipping and believing.

About a hundred individuals and about a dozen institutions have cooperated in compiling the information on these questions gathered in this volume. But central to the work was an institution within Columbia University, known as a University Seminar. This is no conventional seminar but a scheme invented in 1944 by Professor Frank Tannenbaum of the History Department of Columbia University and organized with the help of 18 colleagues and Dr. Frank Fackenthal, then Provost of the University. Each University Seminar is an independent "intellectual community of fellows" gathered from varied professions and institutions for the study of a particular large problem but all are officially approved by Columbia University. After 15 years of operation there were 27 such seminars with a total of over 600 members. The particular University Seminar, out of whose labors this volume has grown, met regularly for 10 years (1948–1958) and was called the Seminar on Inter-religious Relations. After the Seminar had concluded its sessions, the three members who now appear as the editors of this volume, were charged with completing the gathering of relevant information and editing the whole for publication. The editors have enjoyed the assistance of a number of contributors and critics in addition to the cooperation of about thirty members of the Seminar, not all of whom served for the whole term of ten years.

The aim of the Seminar and of this Handbook is strictly one of information, not evaluation. No general conclusions or criticisms are attempted, except those that are embedded in the various contributions to Part III of the Handbook. It is hoped and expected that this Handbook will be a convenient reference work for any institution or individual engaged in dealing with inter-religious problems. Though there are bits of historical orientation here and there as needed, the main body of the work is comprised of three types of contemporary materials gathered from the best sources available.

I. Recent formulations by responsible officials of religious organizations or by acts of their governing bodies, of the principles and policies which have normative force today in defining and regulating the attitude and behavior of their members in relation to members of other religions so far as religious observances or doctrines are concerned.

II. Recent formulations, less official, of such principles and policies by representative spokesmen or leaders of a major religion. In the majority of these religions there is no central authoritative government in these matters, so that it is necessary to rely on what the well-informed, representative leaders of the religion believe to be the guiding principles and policies generally accepted in their religion today as most authoritative and orthodox.

III. Recent attempts by scholarly students of the general problems of inter-religious relations to formulate critical principles for the improvement of inter-religious relations. These essays are concerned not with the point of view of only one religion but with current trends in various religions which suggest possibilities for making the meeting of faiths more peaceful and fruitful. These are not attempts to formulate super-faiths or world religions, but rather to promote the integrity and enlightenment of each religion in a world situation in which all are interacting.

In the *Appendix* there is a bibliography and a directory, of several international organizations which have a direct or indirect concern with problems of inter-religious relations. In several cases it was possible to cite relevant statements authorized by the organizations.

The editors wish to acknowledge in addition to the general indebtedness of the Seminar to Professor Tannenbaum and to Columbia University for making this study possible, their special indebtedness to the many persons who have contributed freely of their time and their information on special topics. Some of them, such as Aziz S. Atiya, Marguerite Block, and Jacques Cuttat, contributed as members of the Seminar; others, notably the Rt. Rev. Msgr. Thomas A. Donnellan, Chancellor at the Archbishopric of New York and several professors of Fordham University; Professor T. M. P. Mahadevan and several heads of ashrams in India, and several Japanese scholars. The Bibliography is largely the work of Professor Ernst Benz and Dr. Minoru Nambara of Marburg; with additional titles supplied by Dr. Bernard Mandelbaum of the Jewish Theological Seminary, New York. Acknowledgment is also due to the Gustav Stern Foundation for its support of the work, and to the Blaisdell Institute of Claremont, California, whose Secretary, Jeannette S. Griggs, prepared final copy for the publisher.

Acknowledgments to publishers for permission to quote from their copyrighted publications is made in footnotes at the appropriate places in the text.

The editors hope that those readers who can make corrections in the text, who have more recent information, or who can in any other way make this Handbook more useful will kindly give us their cooperation toward a prospective second edition. In this field of inter-religious relations, where changes are now taking place rapidly, it is important to have the latest reliable information, and the editors hope to keep the Handbook as up-to-date and reliable as possible.

MOSES JUNG
SWAMI NIKHILANANDA
HERBERT W. SCHNEIDER
Editors

PART ONE

OFFICIAL FORMULATIONS OF NORMS BY CHRISTIAN RELIGIOUS BODIES

(A Selection of the Chief Types)

Roman Catholic
United Lutheran Church in America
World Council of Churches

INTRODUCTION

The materials included in Part I are confined to the Christian Churches and represent the efforts of these churches to legislate on questions of "external relations." The relations here considered are those which involve their members in dealings, not merely with members of other religions, but with other religions themselves; that is, those questions which concern Christians in their attitudes toward other faiths and cults. This excludes inter-religious problems of morals or politics, except as they involve the principles of the relations of one religion to another. The most significant and typical attempts to deal with these questions authoritatively have been made by the Roman Catholic Church, certain Lutheran churches and by the World Council of Churches. The norms formulated by the World Council, through the International Missionary Council are accepted as authoritative by many Protestant and Orthodox bodies, but do not have the force of church law, inasmuch as these churches allow varying degrees of liberty in such matters. What is true of the World Council of Christian churches is even more true of contemporary Oriental, Muslim and Jewish religions which are, for the most part, not subjected to central government in these matters.

Practically all organized religions have authoritative scriptures and recognize in these scriptures an element of law as well as of doctrine. Consequently the ultimate norms and primary sources of contemporary legislation are to be found in such scriptures. There is no attempt made here to review these ancient laws. What concerns us here are the recent attempts to apply such sacred traditions to the contemporary world. The most careful and reflective attempts to formulate general rules for inter-religious conduct and attitudes are to be found in recent pronouncements by the Vatican, the United Lutheran Church of America and the World Council of Churches. These are by no means the only attempts, but they are the most influential and are selected here as typifying various approaches to the problem of inter-religious relations.

ROMAN CATHOLIC CANON LAW AND RECENT
ENCYCLICALS OF THE POPES

I. The Canon Law

The norms regulating the relations of Catholics with non-Catholics in matters of faith and culture are given in the Code of Canon Law of the Church which goes back to the 12th Century and which may be re-codified soon. (see below p. 16) It began to be published in 1909 as *Acta Apostolicae Sedis*. The following excerpts as given in the English Canon Law Digest compiled by T. Lincoln Bouscaren, S.J. (Bruce Publishing Co., Milwaukee, 3 vols.) are canons involving, for the most part, relations with schismatics, but also, some of them, relations with infidels.

Canon 1351

No one is to be forced against his will to embrace the Catholic faith.

Canon 1258 : 1

It is illicit for Catholics in any way to assist actively or take part in sacred worship of non-Catholics.

Canon 1258 : 2

Passive or merely material presence for the sake of civil courtesy, duty, or respect, for a grave reason which, in case of doubt, should have the approval of the Bishop, may be tolerated, at the funerals, weddings, and other such celebrations of non-Catholics, provided there is no danger of perversion or of scandal.

Canon 1325 : 3

Catholics are to avoid disputations or conferences about matters of faith with non-Catholics, especially in public, without the permission of the Holy See or, in urgent cases, permission of the Bishop of the place. (This rule was reasserted in connection with "ecumenical congresses" in 1927, 1928, 1948 and 1949. It was also invoked by Pope Leo XIII when he rebuked Cardinal Gibbons for opening the World's Parliament of Religions at the Chicago World's Fair in 1893 by reciting the Lord's Prayer.) But policy is more lenient in recent permissions to hold private discussions where the aim is "seeking the truth." Canon 1325 was used in 1919 to condemn specifically "joining theosophic societies and reading their publications."

(Canon Law Digest, I, p. 620)

Canon 1324

Regulating "the teaching office of the Church," was the basis for a papal decree of 1928 which abolished a missionary society among Jews called "Friends of Israel," condemned its publication *Pax Super Israel*, as contrary "to the spirit of the Church," and in this connection condemned anti-Semitism as follows: "The Holy See reprobates all hatred and contention among peoples, so especially does it condemn the spirit of hatred against that people once chosen of Almighty God, which is called anti-Semitism. (Canon Law Digest, Vol. I, p. 616.)

Canon 1399 : 3

"Books which have for their principal or one of their notable purposes to attack religion or right morals are forbidden." "The term 'to attack religion' raises a doubt of law. Most authors hold that it means to attack the Catholic religion; others maintain that the attack must be against all religion in order to be condemned. The latter is the less severe opinion and may be followed." (Bouscaren, *Canon Law*, 1951, p. 786).

Canon 399 : 4

"Books by any non-Catholics which treat professedly of religion are forbidden, unless it is certain that they contain nothing against the Catholic faith."

Canon 399 : 7

"Books which teach or approve of any sort of superstition, fortune telling, divination, magic, spiritism or other such practices are forbidden."

Canon 1350

"Missionaries are to avoid efforts to propagate their own national language among the peoples to whom they are sent; they are not to introduce the laws or customs of their own land, especially in the matter of feasts, fast and abstinence; they are not to promote the subordination of the lands where they are working as missionaries to the preponderant power of their own nation; let them abstain from promoting political designs or temporal business of any kind either with their own country or other countries; let them encourage the people to obey the civil authorities; let them carefully observe the provisions of canon 1386 regarding the publication etc., of books, papers, and periodicals, especially on political matters. The mission papers and magazines should reflect zeal for the Kingdom of God, not for the prestige of their own country." (Bouscaren, T.L. *Canon Law Digest – Supplement through 1948*, p. 192)

Instruction on Prudence in Treating of Mission Matters "This Sacred Congregation has more than once observed in periodicals and books concerning the work of the missions as well as in public speeches on the same subject, that the manners, culture, character, and condition of the peoples to whom the Catholic faith is to be brought, are sometimes depicted in such a way as to portray rather their bad than their good traits. Everyone knows, of course, that this is done in no malicious spirit, but rather for the sole purpose of arousing a livelier charity toward brethren who are not yet in possession of the light of Christ, and to provide more aid for them by works of religion and charity. At the same time, if one reflects how he himself would feel if strangers spoke in this way of his own country, it becomes evident that this manner of speaking is quite contrary to mutual courtesy between different peoples, that it is a breach of equity and of justice, and finally that it rightly stirs the people of whom such things are said to no little indignation."

"This way of acting is especially to be entirely avoided for the reason that it may create a false impression, which does an injustice to the missionaries and prejudices the success of their ministry; namely, that they fail to come to the pagan nations with that sincere charity which would enable them, not to judge others by their own standards, but to try openly and sincerely to understand, to esteem, and to love them."

"Accordingly, this Sacred Congregation recommends to all who either write or speak of mission matters, that they do so with the same regard that they would have strangers show in speaking of their own country."

"In this connection they should also remember that not a few of the nations among whom missionary work is being done are distinguished by an ancient and noble civilization and culture, so that they are hurt and angered when they are indiscrimately confused with and held equal to those who, as we say, are less developed. Nor is it right from individual instances to formulate an injurious and false opinion of an entire people." (Bouscaren, T. L., *Canon Law Digest Vol. II*, pp. 420–421)

Pope Pius XII, *Encyclical Evangelii Praecones*

This Encyclical *(Heralds of the Gospel)* was sent out June 2, 1951 as a conclusion of the general revaluation of the missionary work of the Church which was made necessary by the revolution in Asia and Africa after World War II. It was given on the 25th anniversary of the important Encyclical of Pius XI, Rerum Ecclesia, which gave new directives to the mission field after World War I. Significant passages from the earlier encyclical are cited in this encyclical and clearly indicate the kind of problems, political and economic, which were disturbing the "native" churches in mission fields. The need for clarification of church policy toward secular movements and ideologies led to a similar need for clarification of relations toward other religious faiths.

The selections from the 1957 encyclical, *Fidei Donum*, contain the special directives for missions in Africa, and state very clearly that the Church ought to be free of particular cultural limitations and ought to thrive above all peoples and cultures.

In view of the upheavals and dangers of the present time, when not a few peoples are divided by conflicting interests, We consider it very opportune on the present occasion to reiterate Our approval of this work. For missionaries preach to all men the practice of natural and Christian virtues and that brotherly and common fellowship which transcends racial conflicts and national frontiers...

It is in keeping with your apostolate not to be hampered by any national frontiers; for your work which unites you in fraternal cooperation, clearly manifests to all that note of the Catholic Church which rejects discord, flees division, and abhors all disputes which agitate nations and sometimes bring them to utter ruin. We refer to that Christian faith and to universal Christian charity which transcend all opposing camps and national boundaries and reach out to the ends of the earth. They are the motives that spur each one of you on to reach your goal, which is the establishment of the Kingdom of God throughout the whole world.

We gladly avail Ourselves of this 25th anniversary of the Encyclical Letter Rerum Ecclesiae to express Our appreciation of the work which has been accomplished and the great consolation it has given Us, and further to exhort all to go forward with still greater zeal...

It is obvious that the work of the apostolate has adapted itself to the changing conditions and growing needs of our times by employing new and more modern methods...

Though some have tried to separate the children of the Catholic Church from Rome and from this Apostolic See, as though patriotism and loyalty so required, yet Catholics have been and are able to make the fully justified rejoinder that, while they are second to none in the matter of patriotism, they genuinely desire to enjoy a rightful liberty...

There are some shepherds, as you know, Venerable Brethren, who strive to lead away the sheep from his one fold and haven of salvation; you likewise know that this danger is daily growing greater. When We consider before God the immense number of men without the truth of the Gospel, and duly reckon the grave danger that faces many from the prevalence of atheistic materialism or from a certain so-called Christian creed which is infected by the tenets and errors of Communism, we feel the deepest concern and solicitude that nothing be left undone to promote the work of the apostolate throughout the world...

We pray God especially for those missionaries who labor in the interior of Latin America, since We are aware of the dangerous pitfalls to which they are exposed from the open and covert attacks of heretical teaching...

First of all it is to be observed that the person who has been called by God to evangelize distant non-Christian lands, has received a very great and sublime vocation. He consecrates his life to God in order to spread His Kingdom to the farthest ends of the earth. He can apply to himself in a special way those beautiful sayings of St. Paul: "Though we walk in the flesh, we do not war according to the flesh." "To the weak I became weak that I might gain the weak."

He must, therefore, consider the country he is going to evangelize as a second fatherland and love it with due charity. Furthermore let him not seek any earthly advantage for his own country or religious Institute, but rather what may help toward the salvation of souls. Certainly he should dearly love his fatherland and his Order, but the Church should be loved with a still more ardent devotion. And let him remember that nothing will be to the advantage of his own Order that is detrimental to the good of the Church.

Moreover it is necessary that those who are called to this kind of apostolate should not only get the spiritual and intellectual training that befits ecclesiastical students, before going out on the mission field, but should learn in addition those subjects which will be most useful to them when they come to preach the Gospel in foreign lands. Hence they should be given a sound knowledge of languages, especially of those which they will require at some future date. Besides they should be sufficiently instructed in the sciences of medicine, agriculture, ethnography, history, geography, etc.

The object of missionary activity, as all know, is to bring the light of the Gospel to new races and to form new Christians. However, the ultimate goal of missionary endeavor, which should never be lost sight of, is to establish the Church on sound foundations among non-Christian peoples, and place it under its own native Hierarchy...

The Church's aim is not the domination of peoples or the gaining of temporal dominions; she is eager only to bring the supernatural light of faith to all peoples, and to promote the interests of civilization and culture, and fraternal concord among nations...

It is clear that the Church cannot be properly and duly established in new territories, unless all is there organized as time and circumstances require and especially unless a native clergy equal to the need has been properly educated and trained. In this connection We should like to borrow the grave and wise directives of the Encyclical Letter Rerum Ecclesiae: "... While each of you should try to have as large a number of native students as possible, you must further make it your aim to fashion and develop in them sacerdotal sanctity and such an apostolic spirit and zeal for the salvation of their own people that they will be ready to lay down their lives for their fellow-tribesmen and fellow-country-men."

"Suppose owing to war or political upheavals there is a change of government in some missionary territory, and the request is made or a law is passed that the foreign missionaries of a certain country must leave: suppose again a more unlikely case, that the native population raised to a higher degree of culture and political development, in order to gain its freedom, wants to drive out of their territory all governors, armed forces and missionaries belonging to the occupying foreign power and that it cannot do so otherwise than by force. What then, We ask, would be the disaster that would threaten the Church throughout all that territory, unless full provision has been made for the needs of the Christian populace by a network of native priests throughout the whole country?"

We are profoundly grieved as We behold these conditions which Our immediate Predecessor described with almost prophetic vision verified in many parts of the Far East. There what were most flourishing missions ripe for the harvest, are now, alas, reduced to the direst straits. Would that it were permitted Us to hope that the peoples of Korea and China, who are naturally cultured and honorable and have been renowned from early times for their high standard of civilization, may as soon as possible be freed not only from turbulent factions and wars, but from the inimical doctrine which seeks only the things of earth and scorns the things of heaven; and moreover that they may appraise rightly the Christian charity and virtue of foreign missionaries and native priests who strive only to promote the genuine good of the people by their labors and, if necessary, by the sacrifice of their lives.

We return heartfelt thanks to God that in both countries a numerous clergy chosen from among the people has grown up as the future hope of the Church, and that not a few dioceses have been entrusted to the care of native Bishops. That this stage of development should have been reached redounds to the credit of the foreign missionaries...

We therefore desire that there be everywhere erected, as far as possible, associations of Catholic men and women, and also of students, of workers, of artists, of athletes, and other clubs and sodalities, which can be considered the auxiliaries of the missionaries. In the erection and constitution of these organizations, let character, virtue and zeal be preferred to numbers.

It is to be borne in mind that nothing is more efficacious in winning for missionaries the confidence of fathers and mothers than devoted care bestowed upon their children.

Although it is clear that Catholic Action should exercise its influence primarily in promoting the works of the apostolate, its members are not prevented from joining other organizations whose purpose is to reform social and political life according to the principles and teaching of the Gospel; in fact, their participation not only as citizens, but as Catholics also, is a right which they possess and a duty to which they are bound.

Since young men, and those especially who have had the advantage of a classical and liberal education, will direct the course of the future, no one can be blind to the supreme importance of devoting the best of care to elementary schools, high schools and colleges...

As we all know, the educated youth of today will form the governments of tomorrow and the masses will follow their leadership and guidance...

Schools and colleges are moreover especially helpful in refuting the errors which now especially are daily infecting more and more non-Catholic and Communist activities and which are being openly and covertly instilled into the minds of youth.

An equally useful service is the dissemination of timely publications. It is scarcely necessary for Us to dwell at length on this point, for everyone knows how effectively newspapers, magazines, and reviews can be employed either to present truth and virtue in their proper light and inculcate them deeply upon men, or to expose fallacies masquerading under the guise of truth, or to refute certain false opinions which are hostile to religion, or which do great spiritual harm by distorted presentation of vexed social questions...

We also wish at this point to pay the highest tribute of praise to the care taken of the sick, the infirm and afflicted of every kind; We mean hospitals, leprosaria, dispensaries and homes for the aged and maternity

cases, and orphanages. These are to Our eyes the fairest flowers of missionary endeavor; they give us, as it were, a vision of the Divine Redeemer
Himself, who "went about doing good, and healing all that were op-
pressed."

Such outstanding works of charity are undoubtedly of the highest
efficacy in preparing the souls of non-Christians and in drawing them to
the Faith and to the practice of Christianity; besides, Our Lord said to
His Apostles; "Into what city soever you enter, and they receive you...
heal the sick that are therein, and say to them: 'the Kingdom of God is
come nigh unto you.'"

Passing now to another aspect of the subject which is of no less importance, We wish to speak of social reforms demanded by justice and
charity. Whilst the propaganda of Communism, today so widespread, is
really deceiving the minds of the simple and untutored, We seem to hear
an echo of those words of the Divine Savior: "I have Compassion on the
multitude." It is imperative to put into practice with zeal and diligence,
the right principles taught by the Church in this matter. It is imperative
to keep all nations free from those pernicious errors, or, in case they are
already tainted with them, to set them free from these inimical doctrines
which represent the enjoyment of this world as the unique goal to be
attained by men in this mortal life. At the same time, by subjecting
everything to state ownership and control, they reduce the dignity of the
human person almost to zero. It is imperative to proclaim in private and
in public that we are all exiles making our way to our immortal home;
and are destined to eternal happiness, to which truth and virtue must
lead us. Christ is the only real defender of human justice, the only true
consoler of the human misery that in this life is unavoidable.

However, it is the duty of all, as far as possible, to mitigate the distress,
sweeten the sorrow and relieve the anguish of their brethren during this life.

Charity indeed can remedy to a certain extent many unjust social
conditions, but that is not enough. For in the first place, there must be
justice which should prevail and be put into practice...

Let not the Gospel, on being introduced into any new land, destroy or
extinguish whatever its people possess that is naturally good, just or
beautiful. For the Church, when she calls people to a higher culture and
a better way of life, under the inspiration of the Christian religion, does
not act like one who recklessly cuts down and uproots a thriving forest.
No, she grafts a good scion upon the wild stock that it may bear a crop
of more delicious fruit. Human nature, though owing to Adam's fall, it
is tainted with original sin, has in itself something that is naturally

Christian; and this, if illumined by Divine Light and nourished by God's grace, can eventually be changed into true and supernatural virtue.

This is the reason why the Catholic Church has neither scorned nor rejected the pagan philosophies. Instead, after freeing them from error and all contamination, she has perfected and completed them by Christian revelation. So likewise the Church has graciously made her own the native art and culture which in some countries is so highly developed. She has carefully encouraged them and has brought them to a point of aesthetic perfection that of themselves they probably would never have attained. By no means has she repressed native customs and traditions but has given them a certain religious significance; she has even transformed their feast days and has made them serve to commemorate the martyrs and to celebrate the mysteries of the faith...

The herald of the Gospel and messenger of Christ is an apostle. His office does not demand that he transplant European civilization and culture, and no other, to foreign soil, there to take root and propagate itself. His task in dealing with those peoples, who sometimes boast of a very old and highly developed culture of their own, is to teach and form them so that they are ready to accept willingly and in a practical manner the principles of Christian life and morality; principles, I might add, that fit into any culture, provided it be good and sound, and which give that culture greater force in safeguarding human dignity and in gaining human happiness.

Encyclical Fidei Donum, April 21, 1957

We have had the joy of establishing the hierarchy in many countries and of raising many African priests to the fulness of the priesthood, in conformity with the "ultimate purpose" of missionary labor, which is to establish the Church "firmly and permanently among new peoples."...

At a time when the establishment of the hierarchy might erroneously lead one to believe that missionary activity is nearing its end, the "care of all the churches" of the vast African continent fills our soul with anxiety more than ever...

We express Our wish that a task of constructive collaboration may be carried out in Africa; a collaboration free of prejudices and mutual sensitiveness, preserved from the seductions and strictures of false nationalism, and capable of extending to these people, rich in resources and future, the true values of Christian civilization, which have already born so many good fruits in other continents...

At the moment when new structures are being sought – while some run the risk of abandoning themselves to the false seductions of a technical civilization – the Church has the duty to offer to them, in the greatest measure possible, the substantial riches of her doctrine and her life as animators of a Christian social order...

The Africans, who are traversing in a few decades the stages of an evolution which the Western world achieved in the course of several centuries, are more easily upset and seduced by the scientific and technical teaching which is being given to them, as well as by the materialistic influences to which they are subjected. For this reason, situations can produce themselves here and there which would be difficult to amend, and consequently the penetration of Catholicism into souls and society would be impaired...

Colleges and schools must be founded and Christian doctrine taught throughout all grades. Organizations for social action must be established to guide the work of chosen groups of Catholics in the service of society. The Catholic press must be developed in all its forms. Modern techniques for the diffusion of culture must be studied for it is known in our day how important a well-formed and enlightened public opinion is. Above all, attention must be given to the growing development of Catholic Action and to the satisfaction of the religious and cultural needs of a generation which, deprived of sufficient food, might be exposed to the danger of going outside the Church to seek nourishment.

In order to take on these different tasks, the pastors of souls need not only greater means, but also and above all collaborators prepared for these more diverse and therefore more difficult ministries...

Nothing is more foreign to the Church of Jesus Christ than division. Nothing is more harmful to her life than isolation, retiring into oneself, and all the forms of collective egoism which induce a particular Christian community, whatever it may be, to close itself up within itself.

"Mother of all nations and of all peoples as well as of all individuals, Holy Mother the Church" is not and cannot be foreign in any place; she lives, or at least by her nature should live, in all peoples...

II. ENCYCLICAL AD PETRI CATHEDRAM OF POPE JOHN XXIII

June 29, 1959

A few paragraphs from this first Encyclical of Pope John XXIII are cited here as relevant to the external relations of Catholics. They concern: (1) a reassertion of the concept "the true religion" in relation to other religions; (2) an emphasis on the religious obligation of all men to be brothers and to live in peace, freedom, and justice; (3) the plan for a "Code of the Canon Law adapted to modern needs;" (4) advice to missionaries to be peaceful "ambassadors of Christ" and to love their "secondary country with true patriotism."

"There is a certain group who, though they do not deliberately attack the truth, yet by their want of respect for it war against it just as though God did not give us the faculty to seek after and discover it. Acting in this fashion leads to the untenable position that since there is no distinction between the true and the false, all religions are basically true. 'This kind of reasoning,' in the words of our Predecessor quoted above, 'is pointed toward the destruction of all religion, and in particular of the Catholic Faith since, of all religions, this alone is true, and cannot be equated with others without serious injustice.' We would go even farther and state that a failure to distinguish between contraries has only this fatal outcome: an unwillingness to accept or practice any religion. For how can God who is truth have any patience with the carelessness, negligence or laziness of those who completely disregard their obligation of searching for and finding these essential truths."...

"We who are placed above the disagreements between nations, we who embrace all people with equal affection, we who are not motivated by earthly benefits nor by desire of political ascendency, nor by any desires in this present life, seem to be able to be judged with fairness, heard with equanimity by all regardless of national background when we speak on matters of such importance. God created men to be brothers, not enemies. He gave them the earth to be cultivated in the sweat of their brow that everyone might share in its fruits and take from it the necessities of daily existence. The various nations are nothing other than societies of men, that is, of brothers who ought to strive not only for their own individual prosperity, but, bound together in a bond of brotherly love, for the good of all human society."...

"If all, as they should be, are eager for peace and not for war, if they look forward with sincerity of heart toward the peace of brotherhood, then only can governments and the affairs of state be seen in their proper perspective and properly regulated. Herein lies the only possibility of a search for and the adoption of that cooperative planning from which will flow out to the whole family of mankind that unity so universally desired. In the enjoyment of this harmony, individual nations will then discover the proper limits of their freedom and will strive not to destroy others by stepping out of their prescribed limits. This is a unity which is foreign to the minds of those who try to oppress others or who strive to deprive them of their freedom."...

"We therefore beseech all, and in particular, those who are the leaders of nations, to weigh these consequences prudently and carefully in the presence of God, the just Judge. We urge that they be aggreeable and willing to try any path that might result in this necessary unity. For, indeed, this harmonious unity on which, as we have said, rests the betterment of the material prosperity of all people, can be re-established only when, with minds at peace and the rights of all firmly assured, the freedom that is our birthright shines forth everywhere, to the Church, to society as a whole, to each and every individual."...

"When we announced that we intended to hold an Ecumenical Council and Roman Synod and that we intended to prepare a Code of Canon Law adapted to modern needs and to publish a new Code of the same type for the Eastern Churches, it was a source of great pleasure to us to have found so many in agreement with our plans."...

"The outcome of the future Ecumenical Council depends more assuredly on, as it were, a sacred contest of prayer than on human efforts and diligent industry. We lovingly extend this invitation of prayer to God to all those who, though they are not of this fold, reverently worship God and try to follow His commands with good will."...

"In union with Catholics the world over, we repeat these pleas with earnest prayers. This we do, not only because we are motivated by ardent love toward all peoples, but because we are stirred by the humility of spirit in the Gospels."...

II

DECLARATION OF PRINCIPLES CONCERNING THE CHURCH AND ITS EXTERNAL RELATIONSHIPS ADOPTED BY THE UNITED LUTHERAN CHURCH IN AMERICA AT ITS CONVENTION OCTOBER 26, 1920, IN WASHINGTON, D. C.

The immediate context of this Declaration is not the problem of relations of the Lutheran Church with non-Christian religious bodies and doctrines, but rather with (A) the ecumenical movement among Christian Churches and the general problem of church unity; (B) anti-Christian secular tendencies such as atheistic political ideologies and naturalistic philosophies. However, the principles here declared are evidently the same that are applied to problems of inter-religious relations. They emphasize, on the one hand, the dangers of compromizing the Faith and on the other hand, the need for "a spirit of catholicity," for the avoidance of "hostility, jealousy, suspicion or pride, in the sincere and humble desire to give and receive," and for "a cordial recognition to all agreements which are discovered." The Church should always appeal to a conscience which it is her sacred duty to enlighten, patiently and persistently, from the Word of God."

Though the policies of the American Lutheran churches toward the ecumenical movement and toward the World Council of Churches have been modified since 1920, due in part to a reorganization within the Lutheran Church, in part to changes of policy in the World Council of Churches, these inter-church developments (with which this Handbook is not directly concerned) have not called for a reformulation of the general principles here formulated, which still apply to inter-religious relations and are shared by most other churches, Catholic and Protestant.

"Every group of professing Christians in which the Word of God is so preached and the Sacraments are so administered that men are saved therein is truly, partial and imperfect, as it may be, an expression of the one holy Church, inasmuch as it displays the marks of the Church. Therefore, no one group can rightfully claim that it is the one, holy, catholic and apostolic Church in the sense in which these terms have been defined."

"We believe, however, that distinctions must be recognized between one group and another. In making these distinctions, we believe that those groups in which the Word of God is most purely preached and confessed, according to the Holy Scriptures, and in which the Sacraments are administered in the closest conformity to the institution of Christ, will be the most complete expression of the one, holy Church. For this reason it is necessary that, when occasion arises, any such group of Christians shall define its relationship to other groups which also claim the name of Church, as well as to other groups and organizations which do not bear that name."

"This definition of relationships should be framed in the spirit of catholicity. Moved by that spirit, a Church will always be ready:

1. To declare unequivocally what it believes concerning Christ and His Gospel and to endeavor to show that it has placed the true interpretation upon that Gospel and to testify definitely and frankly against error.

2. To approach others without hostility, jealousy, suspicion or pride, in the sincere and humble desire to give and receive Christian service.

3. To grant cordial recognition to all aggreements which are discovered between its own interpretation of the Gospel and that which others hold.

4. To co-operate with other Christians in works of serving love in so far as this can be done without surrender of its interpretation of the Gospel, without denial of conviction, and without suppression of its testimony as to what it holds to be the truth."...

"In view of the prevalence throughout our land of doctrines which are subversive of the Christian faith; and in view of the indifference manifested by many Christian people to the doctrines and principles of the teachers, sects and organizations which seek their adherence and support; and in view of the fact that through the acceptance of religious and other teachings which contradict the Gospel of Christ, the faith of Christians is endangered; we declare.

1. That we solemnly warn all our pastors and the members of our congregations against all teachers, sects and organizations of any kind, whose doctrines and principles contradict the truths set forth in this Declaration, or which limit their adherents or members in a free confession of their Christian faith.

2. That we warn them especially against all teachers, sects and societies whose doctrines and principles deny the reality of sin, the personality of God, the full and complete Godhead of our Lord Jesus Christ, and His redemption of the world by His sufferings and death, and the

truth and authority of the Holy Scriptures; as well as against all teachers, sects, and societies which teach that men can be saved from sin, or can become righteous before God, by their own works or by any other means than the grace and mercy of God in Jesus Christ. We believe that such doctrines are not only not Christian, but are anti-Christian and destructive of true Christian faith and life.

3. That inasmuch as these and other false and dangerous doctrines are widely spread, not only by the activity of individual teachers, but also by the dissemination of literature and through the agency of societies and other organizations, calling themselves by various names which oftentimes conceal the real nature of the doctrines and principles for which they stand; we therefore lay it upon the consciences of the pastors and of the members of all our congregations to scrutinize with the utmost care the doctrines and principles of all teachers, sects, organizations and societies of every sort which seek their adherence and support, and to refuse such adherence and support in all cases of conflict or possible contradiction between these principles and doctrines and those set forth in Holy Scripture and in the Confessions of the Church. In the application of this principle the Church should always appeal to a conscience which it is her sacred duty to enlighten, patiently and persistently, from the Word of God."

III

DELIBERATIONS AND DECLARATIONS
OF THE WORLD COUNCIL OF CHURCHES

George W. Carpenter, the author of this account of recent developments among Protestant Churches in the theory and practice of inter-religious relations is Associate Secretary of the International Missionary Council. He has generously prepared this Survey for this Handbook, in behalf of the World Council of Churches. It is evident that the whole problem is being studied intensively since 1954 by various agencies of the World Council of Churches and that further pronouncements are to be expected. Indicative of the direction in which these studies are moving are the extracts from the reports on the Bossey Discussions in Switzerland early in 1958, which are appended to Dr. Carpenter's account.

No central authority is recognized by Protestant churches as competent to speak on their behalf in matters of faith or practice. Consequently, no authoritative statement is possible on the attitude of Protestantism toward other faiths. However, on many occasions the International Missionary Council, the various national councils of churches, and since its inception in 1948, the World Council of Churches, have made pronouncements which represented a wide consensus of judgment on the part of their member bodies. Such statements "carry only the authority of their inherent wisdom," but their significance is often exceedingly great, not only in defining a position but also as a point of reference for further inquiry and as a focus for a growing unanimity of judgment. It is in this sense that the statements which follow are to be read.

The relation between Protestant Christianity and the non-Christian faiths has been the subject of continuing study by the International Missionary Council for many years. It first finds explicit mention in the findings of the Jerusalem Meeting in 1928. The section on the Missionary Motive contains the following paragraphs:

"The Gospel is the answer to the world's greatest need. It is not our discovery or achievement; it rests on what we recognize as an act of God. It is first and foremost 'Good News'. It announces glorious Truth. Its very nature forbids us to say that it may be the right belief for some but not for others. Either it is true for all, or it is not true at all.

"...We repudiate any attempt on the part of trade or of government, openly or covertly, to use the missionary cause for ulterior purposes. Our Gospel, by its very nature and by its declaration of the sacredness of human personality, stands against all exploitation of man by man, so that we cannot tolerate any desire, conscious or unconscious, to use this movement for purposes of fastening a bondage, economic, political, or social, on any people.

"Going deeper,... we would repudiate any symptoms of a religious imperialism with desire to impose beliefs and practices on others in order to manage their souls in their supposed interests. We obey a God who respects our wills and we desire to respect those of others.

"...We do not go to the nations called non-Christian because they are the worst of the world and they alone are in need; we go because they are a part of the world and share with us in the same human need – the need of redemption from ourselves and from sin, the need to have life complete and abundant and to be remade after the pattern of Christlikeness. We desire a world in which Christ will not be crucified but where His spirit shall reign.

"We believe that men are made for Christ and cannot really live apart from Him. Our fathers were impressed with the horror that men should die without Christ – we share in that horror; we are impressed also with the horror that men should live without Christ...

"Christ is our motive and Christ is our end. We must give nothing less and we can give nothing more."[1]

This quotation represents the consensus of the 1928 meeting, which was reached after a detailed study of the particular relevance of Christianity in relation to Hinduism, Confucianism, Buddhism, Islam, and secular civilization. This inquiry undertook "not to remain within the region of intellectual argument and definition," but to "penetrate into the deeper region of the things by which men live." In other words, it was an attempt to move beyond the traditional field of comparative religion and to examine each of the major religions in terms of its total significance as a formative element in personal and social life. Since 1928 this inquiry has been pressed much further than was then possible. It has been carried to a deeper level by the fact that strong and mature Christian churches now exist within the areas of each of the major faiths. These constitute a living demonstration of the universality which was set forth as a conviction of faith in the 1928 statement and in later pronouncements.

The next world meeting of the International Missionary Council took place at Tambaram, Madras, India, in 1938. By that time the conviction was growing that Christianity itself, as an institutionalized religion largely conformed to the surrounding society, stands under judgment from the standpoint of the purpose of God in the life of the world in precisely the same way as do the non-Christian religions. The Church must be con-

sidered from two aspects. As a human institution it partakes of the frailty
and sin of human nature. In this sense Christianity is one of the religions.
But, at the same time, the Church is also the fellowship of those persons
in whom the new life in Christ is already present. Through them, indi-
vidually and corporately, the knowledge of God and the purpose of God
are mediated to the world. The basic issue at Tambaram was whether the
revelation of God in Jesus Christ is to be regarded as part of a continuum
of religious experiences in which the non-Christian religions also find a
place, or whether the Christian revelation is *sui generis*, standing apart
from the religions as God's unique act of selfdisclosure in human history.
The issue was sharpened by the publication, as a preparatory document,
of "The Christian Message in a non-Christian World," by Hendrik
Kraemer.[2] Although Dr. Kraemer supported the thesis of discontinuity
in a somewhat extreme and provocative manner, his book has become a
classic in its field and is still of great value. The issue was hotly debated
both during the Tambaram meeting and afterward. The somewhat provisional consensus reached during the meeting is expressed in the following excerpt from the findings:

> "Our message is that God was in Christ reconciling the world unto Him-
> self. We believe that God revealed Himself to Israel, preparing the way
> for His full revelation in Jesus Christ, His Son, our Lord. We believe that
> Christ is the Way for all, that He alone is adequate for the world's need.
> Therefore we want to bear witness to Him in all the world.
> "There are many non-Christian religions that claim the allegiance of
> large multitudes. We see and readily recognize that in them are to be found
> values of deep religious experiences and great moral achievements. Yet we
> are bold enough to call men out from them to the feet of Christ. We do so
> because we believe that in Him alone is the full salvation which man needs.
> Mankind has seen nothing to be compared with the redeeming love of God
> in the life and death and resurrection of Christ. What He is for us, judge
> and redeemer, teacher and friend, brother and Lord, we long to see Him
> become also for others.
> "We do not think that God has left Himself without witness in the world
> at any time. Men have been seeking Him through all the ages. Often the
> seeking and longing have been misdirected. But we see glimpses of God's
> light in the world of religions, showing that His yearning after His erring
> children has not been without response. Yet we believe that all religious
> insight and experience have to be fully tested before God in Christ; and we
> see that this is true as well within as outside the Christian Church. Christ
> is revolutionary; He brings conversion and regeneration when we meet
> Him, from whatever point we may have started. Paul says: 'What things
> were gain to me, those I counted loss for Christ.' "[3]

The Tambaram debate gave rise to the publication of a symposium on

"The Authority of the Faith," which appeared as Volume I of "The Madras Series" embodying the reports of the meeting with added material. In the opening essay of this volume, entitled "Continuity or Discontinuity," Dr. Kraemer gives a concise summary of his position. Some of his theses are important, as they represent a point of convergence of much subsequent thinking. He wrote as follows:

"The Christian revelation as the record of God's self-disclosing revelation in Jesus Christ is absolute *sui generis*. It is the story of God's sovereign redeeming acts having become decisively and finally manifest in Jesus Christ, the Son of the Living God, in whom God became flesh and revealed His grace and truth."

"The Bible, the human and in many ways historically conditioned document of God's acts of revelation, consistently testifies to divine acts and plans in regard to the salvation of mankind and of the world, and not to religious experience or ideas. Religious experiences or ideas are, of course, not absent from the Bible... but in no sense whatever are they *central*... The Bible and its contents can only be understood when it is taken as the record of God's thoughts and acts in regard to mankind and not as a tale about the pilgrimage of the human soul toward God."

"Theologically speaking, 'nature,' 'reason' and 'history' do not... afford preambles, avenues or lines of development toward the realm of grace and truth as manifest in Jesus Christ. There are, to be sure, longings and apperceptions in the religious life of mankind... of which Christ... may be termed, *in a certain sense*, the fulfillment. Yet, it is mistaken... to describe the religious pilgrimage of mankind as a preparation ... [For] in this fulfillment is contained a radical recasting of values, because these longings, when exposed to the searching and revolutionary light of Christ, appear to be blind and misdirected... In Christ all things become new because He is the crisis of all religions... God as He is revealed in Jesus Christ is *contrary* to the sublimest pictures we made of Him before we knew Him in Jesus Christ... Mankind in its totality is in a state of hostility toward God as He *really is*.

"[We do not deny] that God has been working in the minds of men outside the sphere of Christian revelation and that there... may be... acceptable men of faith who live under the sway of non-Christian religions, products, however, not of these non-Christian religions but of the mysterious working of God's spirit. God forbid that we mortal men should be so irreverent as to dispose of how and where the sovereign God of grace pure love has to act. Yet, to represent the religions of the world as... a schoolmaster to Christ, is a distorted presentation of these religions and their fundamental structure and tendencies, and a misunderstanding of the Christian revelation. ...Christ 'the Power of God' and 'the Wisdom of God' stands in contradiction to the power and wisdom of man."

"If we take the 'revelation' claimed in different religions, we have to confess that they do not piece together or form an intelligible whole. The

Vedas, the Koran, the Gospel, do not make a coherent scheme. They do not even answer the same questions."

"Christianity as a historical religion has to be distinguished very sharply from the Christian revelation, because Christianity, as the well-known historical phenomenon which belongs to world history and church history, has in very many respects to be put on the same plane as the other religions of mankind. ...The Christian revelation is not only the 'crisis' (judgment) and redemption of the ethnic religions, but is just as much the crisis and judgment of Christianity as a historic religion."

"Sincerely cooperative thinking which passionately aspires after truth... does not mean a hodge-podge of various views, but a courageous wrestling with each other about the most reverent and faithful way to interpret God's mind as it shines in Jesus Christ, our Lord. Therefore... we must abandon the much practiced habit of hurling at each other generalizations about the divine qualities or the God-forsakenness of the non-Christian religions. The problem whether and, if so, where, and in how far, God... has been and is working in the religious history of the world and in man in his quest for goodness, truth, and beauty, is a baffling and awful problem. ...In the light of the Christian revelation... the problem becomes still more baffling and awful, because our thinking has to be done in the spirit of Christ, which involves prophetic frankness and priestly mercifulness and prudence at the same time."[4]

Dr. Kraemer and others who shared in the Tambaram debate were well aware that they were blazing fresh trains into largely unexplored territory. The basic question of the relation of the Christian revelation to the faiths of mankind has been discussed at intervals since the dawn of Christian history. But it is raised with new insistence today because modern communications have annihilated distance and because the secular world view has challenged *all* the religious presuppositions of mankind. Since 1938 the trail has been broadened and the original presumptions tested by encounters with many fresh situations. World War II has deepened the realization that mankind is a unity, sharing the same nature, the same needs, and the same lostness. The pseudo-religion of Communism has been added to the number of rival faiths which challenge the claims of Christianity. The Whitby meeting of the International Missionary Council in July, 1947, recognized that Christianity must establish its validity not in respect to this or that competing faith but in respect to human nature itself. Its task is therefore much the same in the "post-Christian" western world as in the areas where other historic faiths hold sway.

"There is a recalcitrance in the mind of man to accept the message of the Gospel, even when it is most clearly set forth; he has an inveterate tendency to modify it, to make it a little more congenial to his own established ways of thought."

"The mind of man is not empty. It is filled with ideas, thoughts and aspirations. Unless the Gospel can be seen as relevant to his condition, it will awaken no response. Unless it can be shown that men's problems have already been considered in the Christian revelation, and a better answer indicated than that which they have thought out for themselves, there will be little inducement to leave ancient ways of thought. Unless it can be made clear that what the Gospel offers to meet the highest and purest of all men's aspirations is far higher than the best they can conceive – to put it in plain language, that the kingdom of God made real in Christ is far more satisfying than the kingdom of man devoutly believed in and proclaimed by the Communist – there is no hope that the Gospel will verify itself as the power of God unto salvation in the present age."[5]

This task was further defined at the Willingen meeting of the International Missionary Council in 1952.

"The Church is sent into every inhabited area of the world. No place is too far or too near... the Church is sent into every political, social and religious community of mankind, both to those near at hand and to those far off. Faithfulness to Christ will require the church to come to grips with the social, political, economic and cultural life of the people to whom it is sent. ...The Church is sent to proclaim Christ's reign in every moment and every situation. ...The Mission of the church will always transcend boundaries, but these can no longer be identified with national frontiers, and certainly not with any supposed line between the 'Christian West' and the 'non-Christian East.' The mission involves geographical extension and also penetration of all spheres of life."[1]

The Second Assembly of the World Council of Churches, at Evanston, Illinois in August, 1954, reached substantially the same conclusions in its consideration of the evangelistic dimension of the life of the Church.

"Without the Gospel the world is without sense, but without the world the Gospel is without reality. Evangelism is no specialized, separable or periodic activity, but is rather a dimension of the total activity of the church. Everything the church does is of evangelizing significance. Through all the aspects of its life the church participates in Christ's mission to the world, both partaking of the Gospel and seeking to communicate it. ...Wherever Christians find themselves separated by caste, class, racial or other barriers, they will boldly cross them, manifesting Christ's solidarity with the whole of mankind. In a divided world they will fulfill Christ's ministry of peace, manifesting in their own life the new mankind which has begun in Jesus Christ. Wherever they encounter social injustice, they will do battle for its redress, bearing witness to the restoration of humanity in Christ."[7]

With more direct reference to the non-Christian faiths, the report states:

"The renascence of non-Christian religions and the spread of new ideologies necessitate a new approach in our evangelizing task. In many countries, especially in Asia and parts of Africa, these religious revivals are reinforced by nationalism and often present themselves as effective bases for social reform. It is not so much the truth of these systems of thought and feeling which makes appeal, but rather the present determination to interpret and change oppressive conditions of life. Therefore they confront us not only as reformulated creeds but also as foundations for universal hope. Such hope is based on man's persistent desire to be master of his own destiny. The gospel hope, on the contrary, does not rest upon what man can do for himself but on God's promise, in judgment and mercy, finally to fulfil His purposes..."

"The ambassador of Christ is primarily concerned not with the faith that a man professes, though he should understand it with sympathetic insight, but with him as he really is, a sinner like himself and one for whom Christ died. ..."

"...The gospel is not the emergence of a new ideal in man, but the entrance of a new power from God into the world. It must, therefore, be proclaimed in the context of power in action. The seeds of the Kingdom are not words and arguments but the children of the Kingdom themselves, scattered and sown in the field of the world."[8]

Since Evanston efforts to reach a more profound understanding of the significance of the Christian gospel to persons of every faith have been carried forward by the Department of Missionary Studies, which is a unit both of the World Council of Churches and of the International Missionary Council. These efforts include two aspects. The first centers in a number of study centers or institutes in various parts of Asia. These serve as focal points for that more intense study of the total significance of the non-Christian faiths and of the relevance of the Christian Gospel in relation to them to which reference has been made in several of the statements quoted above. The second is a study being carried forward by the staff and committee of the Department of Missionary Studies on the theme of "The Word of God and the Living Faiths of Mankind." Concurrently with this study another one has been undertaken by the Department of Evangelism of the World Council of Churches. This faces many of the same questions from the standpoint of the task of the churches in their local environment. These studies are still in process of development, and it would be premature to predict results at this stage.

The Bossey Meeting on "The Word of God and the Living Faiths of Men"

(Excerpts from the "World Council of Churches, Division of Studies, Bulletin Vol. IV, No. 1, April 1958)

When the Central Committee at its meeting at Galyatetö, Hungary, in 1956 authorized the Department of Missionary Studies and the Department of Evangelism jointly to undertake a study on "The Word of God and the Living Faiths of Men", it provided for the appointment of a committee to guide the study. A committee drawn from member churches in Asia, Europe and North America under the chairmanship of Dr. David G. Moses was constituted. The committee has had to function by correspondence during the past year, but a first meeting of members was held at the Ecumenical Institute, Bossey, from March 14th to 18th.

The Bossey meeting took place against the background of a consultation on the relationship of Christianity and the non-Christian religions held at Davos in Switzerland in 1955 which was in the nature of a *ballon d'essai*. The stated purpose of the Davos consultation was to revive the "Tambaram Debate" of 1938. This debate about the relationship of Christianity and the non-Christian religions which one associates with the Madras or Tambaram meeting of the International Missionary Council and the name of Professor Hendrik Kraemer had lapsed, partly because of the rapid onset of the war and the preoccupations of the succeeding years. The issues involved in it, however, had not been resolved, but if anything, had become more crucial. It was clearly realized at Davos (and this was the main value of the consultation) that a great deal more was required than a revival of an old debate which had its own setting, terms, and personalities. At Davos and during the past year a good deal of thought has been given to understanding the new setting of studies in the relationship of Christianity and the non-Christian religions...

In a fundamental respect the discussion at Bossey differed from earlier discussions of Christianity and the non-Christian religions. To put it simply, they did not oppose Christianity and the non-Christian religions as such to one another, but made a basic distinction between the Gospel and all religions. This distinction presupposed that the important point of concern is not with religious systems as such but with religious man and especially with men under the proclamation of the Gospel. The important result of this distinction is that the starting point is anthropological, that it is with man – however conditioned by his religion and history and environment. Thus in the first instance at any rate, the problems of the comparisons of truths of one system with truths of another are transcended because the center of attention is not these truths but the human being himself...

In the present age man's traditional conception of the classical religions is undergoing considerable if not radical change. In part this is due to (1) the great impact of Western civilization and the desire which all countries have for their own economic and industrial development. In part it is due to (2) the need with which newly developed countries are confronted to find an ideology by which they may live. In part it is due to (3) the encounter of one religion with another, an encounter which has been brought about in large measure by the missionary activity of the Christian Church. In part it is due to (4) the realization that religion in its traditional form is being challenged by modern civilization and is in danger of being outmoded, and to a desire to preserve and re-interpret those beliefs and values which are claimed as abiding and are considered to be the only hope of saving the world from swift and final disintegration and destruction.

In their renewed form many religions claim a world mission which is being pursued with vigour, particularly in the West.

It is these "living faiths" in this new situation which must be studied and it is to man living in these faiths that the Word of God must be addressed.

PART TWO

STATEMENTS BY REPRESENTATIVES OF RELIGIOUS BODIES CONCERNING THE PRINCIPLES AND POLICIES

GOVERNING RELATIONS WITH OTHER RELIGIONS

CHAPTER ONE

BUDDHISM

PUJJIAH NARADA MAHA THERA

The Attitude of Buddhism Toward Other Religions

The author of this statement is Chief Priest of the Vajirarama Temple of Theravada Buddhism, Aramapura Sect, Colombo, Ceylon.

> "Concourse alone is best, that is, all should hearken willingly to the doctrines professed by others." – Asoka, Toleration Edict

Buddhism is not a religion based on the fear of the unknown, but a moral and philosophical system based on beliefs that can be tested and verified by experience. Its founder, the "Buddha" which means an A-wakened or Enlightened One, was not a Divine Saviour, nor a prophet, nor an incarnation of a God, but a wonderful man, a unique teacher. He was not born a Buddha, but became one by his own efforts and wisdom. Without claiming the monopoly of Buddhahood, he exhorted others to emulate him and expounded the method to attain that state of perfection.

Anybody who aspires to become a Buddha is termed a Bodhisatta, literally a wisdom-being. This Boddhisatta ideal, exclusively Buddhistic, is the most beautiful and most refined course of life that can ever be conceived of in this ego-centric world; for what is nobler than a life of service and purity. In Catholicism the Boddhisatta has been canonized as St. Josaphat and in Hinduism the Buddha is venerated as an incarnation (avatāra) of the God Vishnu.

Since Buddhism is not regarded as a revealed religion owing any allegiance to a Supreme Being, it neither claims the monopoly of truth nor condemns any other religion. Unfair criticism of other faiths is denounced in Buddhism.

It must, however, be admitted that in Buddhism are found teachings both similar and dissimilar to the fundamental tenets of other world religions. The attitude of Buddhism toward all world religions is absolutely friendly; but it does not assert that all religions lead to the same goal and that all faiths are different interpretations of one supreme Truth. Nevertheless, with no feelings of separatism or antagonism, Buddhism wholeheartedly cooperates with all religions in both worldly and spiritual matters that tend to the weal and happiness of mankind. Buddhism is universal and supernational. Buddhist *Metta* or lovingkindness unites all, irrespective of caste, class or creed, colour or sex. Akin to loving-kindness in Buddhism are non-violence in Hinduism, Jainism and Zoroastrianism, neighborliness in Judaism and Christianity and brotherhood in Islam. If, on account of their respective beliefs, peoples of different faiths cannot meet on a common platform like brothers and sisters, then surely the missions of all religious teachers have pitifully failed.

Buddhism is rational, non-aggressive and extremely tolerant. To its credit it should be said that during its eaceful march of more than 2500 years no drop of blood was shed in the cause of Buddhism. Aldous Huxley remarks: "Alone of all the great world religions, Buddhism made its way without persecution, censorship or inquisition." Buddhists are so tolerant that no foreign missionaries ever experienced any difficulty in propagating their faiths peacefully in predominantly Buddhist lands. In some countries Buddhists have generously granted ideal sites for the erection of churches. Buddhists feel righteous resentment only when repulsive methods are used.

Buddhism not only tolerates other faiths but also judiciously adopts healthy features and effective measures of other systems without modifying its own fundamentals. Buddhists, for instance, have successfully imitated Christians in establishing Young Men's Buddhist Associations, Young Women's Buddhist Associations and Buddhist Sunday Schools. Buddhists are no slaves either to a book or an individual. There is complete freedom of thought and action. Excommunications and ostracisms for any reason whatever are foreign to Buddhism. Though later by conviction they embraced Buddhism, the husband of Visakha, the chief benefactress of the Buddha, and a son-in-law of Anathapindika, the chief supporter of the Buddha, were non-Buddhists. The Buddha raised no objections to their marriages on account of their religious beliefs.

In Theravada Buddhism, men are not regarded as sinners to be saved by a Divine Saviour. Not being sinners, Buddhists do not expect salvation by mere faith in a Saviour or God. As such, Buddhism is not a religion of devotion but an energetic *Middle Path of Enlightenment* which avoids extremes. It emphasizes the importance of self-exertion and self-reliance and states that both purification and defilement depend upon oneself. Instead of petitionary prayers, superstitious rites, ceremonies, sacrifices and penances, meditation plays a great part in this unique path. Meditation is exalted in Hinduism. Contemplative Christian monks and ascetics of other faiths also practice meditation in their own way. This Middle Way is "the only path" for purification and deliverance from suffering.

Many religions try to rationalize suffering while Buddhism accepts suffering as a fact and attempts to eliminate it by removing the cause. In doing so, Buddhism denies the existence of a Creator who controls the destinies of mankind, and advances the doctrine of Karma, the law of moral causation, to solve the problem of suffering and the inequality of mankind. This law of Karma is also taught in Hinduism; and the Biblical saying, "As thou sowest, so shalt thou reap, may be interpreted as this law of moral cause and effect. Karma and its corollary, the doctrine of Rebirth, are common to both Buddhism and Hinduism. Hinduism teaches reincarnation; Buddhism teaches rebirth. According to the former a permanent soul comes into flesh again. The latter denies an immortal soul and posits a dynamic flux. This no-soul doctrine is a distinct characteristic of Buddhism and so is the doctrine of Nibbana, the extinction of craving and suffering, the ultimate goal of Buddhism. This *summum bonum* is to be achieved in this life and is not a union with a Divine Essence or a God in an after-life.

KŌSHŌ OHTANI

The Attitude of Buddhism Toward Other Religions

The author is Chief Abbot of the Nishi Honganji, Kyoto, a monastery of the Shinshu Sect of Māhāyana Buddhism. This statement applies to Japanese Buddhism specifically and to its attitude toward other religions, but the opening paragraphs apply to Buddhism in general.

The saintly Āryadeva, who was active in the first half of the third century in India, was a disciple of the famous Nagarjuna, the great scholar of the Madhyamaka school of Māhāyana Buddhism. He embodied well in his own person his teacher's doctrines, which emphasized void (sūnyata) and selflessness (anātman); and in his own life he carried these teachings out in practice. The extreme zeal of his missionary endeavors earned him the enmity of persons of other religions, who dispatched an assassin against him and had him murdered in the mountains. In his final moments, Āryadeva turned to the man who had fatally stabbed him and said:

"I have fallen the victim of this misfortune because of inevitable karma originating in my own self. I bear no hatred toward you. Hatred cannot be vanquished by hatred, but only by love, entirely free of hate. This is the Buddha's teaching."

This historical fact shows us that the practice of *sūnyata* and *anātman*, the two most fundamental principles of Buddhism, is nothing but the concrete embodiment of a tolerant compassion which abandons selfish attachments and forgives all with a warm, all-embracing love.

It is definitely true that the spirit of Buddhism has at its basis a tolerance which, while subjecting all things to sharp criticism, nevertheless strives to accept them all on their own terms. For this reason, Buddhism, as a rule, does not assume an exclusive attitude of rejection toward other religions, but rather seeks to absorb and embrace them. This can be immediately understood when viewing the broad, all-embracing spirit of such a representative scripture as the *Saddharma-pundarīka-sutra*.

Japanese Buddhism has also traditionally accepted and realized this tolerant spirit peculiar to Buddhism. One can surmise this from the very fact that this *Saddharma-pundarīka-sutra* was the predominant scripture continuously from the introduction of Buddhism into Japan until at least the medieval period. It was largely on the authority of the doctrines of this scripture that the Japanese Buddhists absorbed and embraced Shinto, the native Japanese religion, within Buddhism, making use of the so-called Honji-suijaku theory, a teaching peculiar to Japanese Buddhism. Shinto, thus, without any conflict or antagonism with Buddhism, was placed in the position of, so to speak, a supplement, an auxiliary of Buddhism.

When Christianity first came to Japan in the sixteenth century, the Japanese government of the time misunderstood it, taking it as a tool of European powers in plotting territorial aggression, and for this reason created a controversy by suppressing it. However, there is hardly any evidence to show that Buddhists ever departed from their time-honored standpoint and actively rejected or excluded Christianity. Consequently, when the newly-formed Meiji government repealed the restrictions against Christianity, Christian missionary work could be started in Japan without resistance or rejections on the part of the Buddhists. Subsequently, up to the present day, there has never been any trouble between the two religions.

But a word must be added to the effect that, though Buddhism is tolerant toward other religions, it is not so in an uncritical manner. Buddhism does not necessarily affirm superstitions and irrational cults which are contrary to science. It is the task of Buddhism to strive to criticize these superstitions and cults, to point out their errors and to lead people to true religion.

In other words, Buddhism, as its basic attitude, vigorously criticizes cults based on superstition and warns people against entering the wrong path; but toward religion which is not degraded by superstitious cults, one can say that Buddhism does not adopt an attitude of exclusion and conflict. Instead, it admits other standpoints, adopts a tolerant attitude toward them, and grants them their appropriate places.

DAISETZ T. SUZUKI

Buddhism and Other Religions

Dr. Daisetz T. Suzuki has interpreted, especially to the West, the intuition of Rinzai Zen Buddhism. This School forms a direct contrast to the philosophical, rational thought of Shinran and Dogen Schools of Buddhism. Dr. Suzuki has referred to Zen Buddhism as "the embodiment of Chinese and Indian thought happily amalgamated, which swayed China from the early T'ang to the late Ming, for about nine hundred years."

The attitude of Buddhism toward other religious teachings will, as far as I can see, be along the following lines:

As we all know, the teaching of Buddhism, whatever its variegated colorings, centers around Buddha's experience known as Enlightenment (*anuttara-samyak-sambodhi*) in Sanskrit and *satori* in Japanese). What determines all Buddhist activities, whatever form or pattern they may take, is controlled by the contents of this experience. Some of the most vital contents are:

1. There is in it no external and historical God as is featured in the Biblical story as creator of the world with all things in it. If the word God happens to appear in Buddhist writings, it carries quite a different meaning, and naturally creation and other myths are interpreted accordingly.
2. Thus it follows that in Buddhism there is no personal agent who gives "commands" of any nature to human beings who are punishable should the commands be somehow violated. Buddhists would say we punish ourselves if punishment is due.
3. The "commands" which Buddhists observe are not something that has come upon them from any outside source; they are the natural outgrowth of a communal life we human beings carry on.
4. If Buddhists are ever told to love the enemy as an injunction or a command as coming from a supernatural being, they would declare, "In the Buddhist experience there is no enemy to hate or to love as such."

5. If they are urged to "crucify" their ego, they may wonder what is meant by "ego" for they have no such ego and its "crucifiction" has no sense whatever. Buddhism upholds the doctrine of no-ego *(nirātma)*.
6. The same may be said about seeking "immortality." Buddhists do not know what it means. In their experience there is no birth-and-death (sāmsāra), hence no "immortality" which is to be sought as something specifically desirable. "We are immortal as we are," they would declare.

From these summary statements, we can see that in the Enlightenment experience there is no "God", no "creator" who gives "commands", no "ego-soul", no "crucifixion", no "resurrection", no dichotomous distinction of good and evil, of friends and foes, and further, there is in Enlightenment no "paradise" to lose, no "judgment" to give, no "immortality" to attain, no "savior" to accept, and no "kingdom" to enter.

Some may ask: Is Buddhism then altogether nihilistic, atheistic, ultra-latitudinarian, ignoring all moral laws and normative principles? If it is to be so characterized, in what relationship does Buddhism stand toward other religions?

The following is my answer:

1. In a word, the central experience of Buddhism is *Śūnyatā* (emptiness) in which all contradictions are identified, all opposites have no meaning. Thus it has neither friends nor foes, no gods, no devils, no goods, no evils. But it is crucial to note that it is because of this absolute *Śūnyatā* (zero) this world of infinite possibilities evolves. Here the Christian idea of God creating out of nothing may be accepted by Buddhists as well. But the latter would go on to add: Zero is infinity and infinity is zero, or being is becoming and becoming is being. This experience, psychologically speaking, is love, absolute love, where enemies and friends have no relevant meaning. Buddhists call this absolute love *mahāprajñā* + *mahākarunā*, which is roughly or only tentatively translatable as "absolute transcendental wisdom + absolute compassion."

   When Buddhism is said to teach sūnyatā (emptiness or "zero=infinity"), the above interpretation is to be understood. Those who would take *Śūnyatā* for sheer nothingness in its relative sense are committers of an error of the grossest and most inexcusable kind.
2. That Buddhists have the cleanest record of peace, tolerance and non-violence in the history of religion shows that they have followed the spirit of their teaching that grew out of Buddha's inner experience. For the same reason, wherever Buddhists went, they never resorted to deeds of exterminating their rival faiths. They not only tolerated but assimilated them in their body. They knew that however irrational,

irrelevant, or even atrocious some faiths may appear, they contain something of truth in them as long as they are genuine out-bursts of a sincere human quest after ultimate reality. Buddhists will always maintain this attitude towards other religious teachings. Christians say "in my Father's house are many rooms." Buddhists would continue: "Being so, let each of us occupy one of them and render the other occupants whatever help they may need and harmoniously and happily and comfortably live together, trusting that the "Father", whoever or whatever he may be, is love, that is *mahāprajñā + mahākaruṇā.*"

3. We must, however, remember that the above remarks do not hinder Buddhists from freely criticizing other religions in regard to their historical development, their doctrinal weaknesses, their one-sided exclusivism, their contribution to a world culture, and the like.

4. Thus, the Buddhist relationship to other faiths or religions is always characterized by this spirit of tolerance and broad-mindedness and co-operation as seen in its history. Undoubtedly, Buddhism will continue to exercise this all-comprehensive spirit of friendliness in whatever situation it may find itself.

HAJIME NAKAMURA

Buddhist Accomodation to Neighboring Religions

Professor Nakamura teaches Indian and Buddhist Philosophy at the University of Tokyo. His following statement is based on his fuller exposition of "Unity and Diversity in Buddhism" published in *The Path of the Buddha. Buddha Interpreted by Buddhists.* Edited by Kenneth W. Morgan. The Ronald Press, New York, 1956.

It is very difficult to have a firm conviction and at the same time to be tolerant, but the Buddha himself and many of his followers have achieved such tolerance. Buddhists are generally noted for their liberal attitude toward other religions, whether polytheistic, monotheistic, or non-theistic. This feature is found in all Buddhist countries. Buddhists admit the truth of any moral and philosophical system, whether primitive or developed, provided only that it is capable of leading men at least part way toward their final goal.

Buddhism has tolerated the other faiths native to the countries in Asia without any clear doctrine of paganism. In Theravada countries, i.e. Ceylon, Burma, Cambodia, Thailand and Laos, many Hindu gods have been included in the religious ceremonies of the Buddhist community, and many Buddhists still observe festivals and customs associated with Nats and other nature spirits of each country. In China, Buddhism has actually been amalgamated with many Taoist beliefs and practices; many shrines are semi-Buddhist and semi-Taoist. The same tolerance has brought about a blending of the various Buddhist sects in China until they are indistinguishable today. In Tibet, Shantarakshita (c. 680–740), the Indian monk who virtually established Lamaism in Tibet, compromised with the Bon religion by incorporating many of its gods and goddesses into the lowest grade of Tantric Guardian Deities without affecting the doctrinal integrity of Buddhism. He replaced the animal sacrifices at the Bons with symbolic worship and taught inner purification in place of black magic. The method was in accordance with the tolerant attitude of the Buddha.

In Japan the indigenous gods and goddesses were dealt with in the same way that they were in Tibet. For about two centuries after the introduction of Buddhism into Japan, they were assigned rather low positions, but from the Heian era, i.e. 794 A.D. onward, their positions became gradually higher and higher; they were regarded as incarnations of Buddhas or Boddhisattvas. Nowadays the common people do not distinguish between Buddhistic divine beings and Shinto gods. In the past in Japan there were very few shrines that did not have shrine temples built in their confines where Buddhist priests followed the morning and evening practices of reciting Sutras and served the shrine gods and goddesses together with Shinto priests. The majority of the Japanese pray before the Shintoist shrines and at the same time pay homage at the Buddhist temples, without being conscious of any contradiction. Many of the better families of Japan send their children to Christian schools in order to have them learn Western culture, although they still continue to be Buddhist.

The above-mentioned attitude is based upon the fundamental standpoint of Early Buddhism. Gotama Buddha refused to give a definite answer on any metaphysical problem which was discussed in those days. He wanted not to be involved in metaphysical disputes. According to him, the various views of other religions and philosophies are nothing but a partial apprehension of the whole absolute which lies beyond our area of cognition. The thought that in spiritual matters we are at best blind beggars fighting with each other in our native darkness is not conducive to a narrow and fanatical bigotry. We should respect each other. This is why Buddhism has been filled with the spirit of tolerance. Buddhism can be regarded as a world religion which has spread, not by force, but by persuasion alone.

CHAPTER TWO

CONFUCIANISM AND CHINESE RELIGIONS

CHUN I. T'ANG

Chinese Attitudes toward World Religions from a Confucianist Point of View

The author is Dean of New Asia College, Hong Kong. Though he stresses the prevalence of the Confucian traditions among the Chinese, he also indicates the inter-relations of Chinese Taoism and Buddhism with Confucianism.

Before I discuss the Chinese attitude toward religions, I wish to cite two sayings, one of Mencius and one of Lu Chiu Yuan, as an introduction to the subject. Mencius said: "The homes of sages may be more than a thousand miles apart and the age of one sage may be a thousand years later than that of another, but the principles of the early sage and the later sage are the same." Lu Chiu Yuan said: "The universe is my mind and my mind is the universe. If in the eastern sea there were to appear a sage, he would have this same mind and this same principle. If in the western sea there were to appear a sage, he would have this same mind and this same principle. If in the southern or northern seas, there were to appear sages, they too would have this same mind and this same principle. If a hundred or a thousand generations ago, or a hundred or a thousand generations hence, sages were to appear, they, likewise, would have this same mind and this same principle." (Cited in Fung Yu-Lan, A History of Chinese Philosophy. Vol. II p. 573. Tr. Derke Bodde, Princeton University Press 1953.)

Mencius and Lu Chiu Yuan were both Confucian. Confucian teaching is mainly ethical; however, it has its religious aspect. The foregoing quotations and what is implied therein can be taken as still representative of the attitude toward religions of the Confucianists and even of the Taoists, the Chinese Buddhists and the Chinese people as a whole.

The significance of these sayings is simple: a principle that is really universal should be universally and immanently presented and realized by human minds of different ages and places. Religious principles are no exceptions. Of course, the religious principle may be revealed by the transcendent God or Heaven. But, at least in the moment of its revelation, what is transcendent must reveal its transcendence to a human mind. Its transcendence cannot transcend the human mind though this mind becomes self-transcendent in that revelation. In this sense, what is transcendent is at the same time immanently revealed to the human mind which is as divine as it is human. Therefore, the really universal principle in religion is not only a universal by itself, but also a universal which can be universally and immanently revealed and then presented or realized by any human mind. Only during the time when it is actually presented and realized by human minds in different ages and places, can its universality be actually revealed to this world and exist in this world. The human minds in which God or Heaven and his principle are revealed, presented and realized are called the minds of the sages. The God or Heaven and his principle may be one and the same, but the minds of the sages are as many as the sages themselves and all men who are capable of being sages, so that one and the same truth can reveal its universality, actually, in the many and different minds.

What Mencius and Lu Chiu Yuan said and its significance as I have explained it, may not be consciously recognized by the ordinary Chinese, yet this is the very essence of the Chinese attitude toward religion. This attitude can be illustrated socially and historically. In Chinese society, individuals are not easily persuaded to think that God is simply incarnated in a physical body at a particular time and place. Nor are most Chinese inclined to believe that there are chosen persons who are predestined to be sages or prophets, and that there are others predestined to be excluded from the Grace of God and ignorant of God. It appears strange to a Chinese, when he is told that only one religion is revealed and the other religions are but natural. The Chinese usually think that if the rain and sunshine of Heaven are present everywhere, if God loves all human beings equally, and if human nature is essentially the same, then there seems no reason for any people to claim the privilege of being a chosen people or to claim that the universal God has been incarnated in a particular body and has revealed his truth only to a particular people or church. The Chinese prefer to believe that "the full realization of human nature in a sage is at the same time the realization of Heaven-nature and the realization of Heaven-mind or God-mind to men," that "all men can be sages and sages are as divine as they are human," and that "all religions are only different expressions of the deepest human nature and at the same time the different channels where the mandates of Heaven flourish or the different ways (Taos) by which different people attain their sagehood and likeness or conformity to Heaven."

The belief that different religions are different ways of attaining sage-hood, all conforming to Heaven, implies that the absolute destination of all the ways may be the same, but that no one way is itself absolute. A "Way" also implies a deeper insight: when a man has traveled the Way and arrived, he can afford to forget the way. Men need not ask others who are also going home whether all "home" is in the same place. If we mean by "home" the same destination of human life – sagehood – then we may say that whoever is already at home should remain at home to entertain the guests coming from different directions and he should never reproach the guests for not coming by the way he came.

The historical evidences for what I have said are plentiful. For example, there have never been religious wars and only a few religious persecutions in Chinese history. The controversies among the Buddhists, the Taoists and the Confucianists in Chinese history usually culminated in a theory of reconciliation among the three teachings or of syncretism and mutual respect, each teaching performing a different function. The metaphor of three rooms in a home, used by the Confucian Wang Lung Chi is apt and significant. It is not an exaggeration to say that the Chinese people in the past have found genuine enjoyment in religious toleration and religious freedom. However, too much religious toleration may weaken one's re-ligious enthusiasm and may result in the absence of religious fervor. We must confess that this, too, is the case among the Chinese.

If we agree that the Chinese are most tolerant in religion, then we shall see why the most tolerable, the most liberal, and the most broad-minded religions are most convincing to the Chinese mind and most heartily welcomed by the Chinese people.

In Chinese history, Buddhism, Islam, Judaism, Nestorianism, Catho-licism, Protestantism and recently, Hinduism, have had followers. But the religion that is most deep-rooted in the lower class Chinese remains Taoism, though it is usually neglected by contemporary Chinese intel-lectuals. Taoism is a religion derived from Chinese primitive religion and is a variable mixture of Taoist philosophy, Confucian teachings and Buddhist beliefs. What appeals most to the Chinese people is its love of longevity and its syncretism, which is a vague, synthetic expression of Chinese liberal spirit, though the spiritual level of Taoists may not be as high as those of Buddhists or Confucians.

Buddhism, expecially Mahayana Buddhism, is a religion widely accept-ed by different classes, including highly intellectual Chinese. The liberal spirit and broad mind of Buddhism is expressed, not by its syncretism, but within the Buddhist teaching itself, Generally speaking, in Buddhist teaching, every sentient being has a "Buddha-nature" and is capable of being a Buddha; and there are different and convenient ways for spiritual cultivation, adapted to different circumstances and different mentalities. Actually there are no, or very few, dogmas in Buddhist teaching. The Chan School or Zen Buddhism, created by the Chinese, even rejected all kinds of articulate preaching and used words simply as tools for the self-awakening of the mind to its own nature. This is close to the idea of "realization of human nature" in Confucian teaching; hence the flourishing of Chan Buddhism in Chinese culture is not an accident.

In contrast to Taoism and Buddhism, Islam and Judaism have practically no followers outside the Muslim and Jewish peoples. This fact is not due to any defect in their teachings when compared with other religions, but to the fact that it is said that Mohammed preached with the Koran in one hand and a sword in the other. This story terrified the Chinese people and they suspected that Islam is narrow minded, although actually this is not the case. As to Judaism, the Biblical idea of Israel as a "chosen people" has been repulsive to the Chinese people. Yet the historical fact that Jews who came to China in the T'ang Dynasty were wholly assimilated with the Chinese people is significant. It is well known that Jews are difficult to assimilate. It is not improbable that the Jews of the T'ang Dynasty were influenced by the liberal spirit of the Chinese people and that their sense of belonging to a chosen people gradually melted away.

The Chinese attitude toward Christianity is rather complicated. It seems to be something between their attitude toward Taoism and Buddhism on one side and their attitude toward Islam on the other.

Christianity is admired by Chinese because it is a religion for all men and not simply the religion of a single folk. According to Christianity, all men who follow the ways of Jesus Christ can be saved. In this sense, it is broad-minded. When Jesuits first came to China in the Ming Dynasty, their erudition in Chinese classics and their writings on the similarities between ancient Confucianism and Christianity won the hearty respect of the Chinese and a number of Chinese became devoted converts to Christianity. Unfortunately, in the Ching Dynasty, the Pope of Rome ordained that Chinese Catholics be forbidden to join in the sacrificial ceremonies for their ancestors or for Confucius and other sages. The Chinese Emperor was irritated by this ruling and ordained that Catholic missions be forbidden in China. So the intolerance of an emperor toward the Catholics was in fact a reciprocal response to the intolerance of a pope. Thus the contact of China with the western world was interrupted for almost two hundred years.

When the Westerners came to China again two hundred years later, the forerunners were then not gentle churchmen but merchants and warriors. Since the Opium War, China has been compelled to make many contacts with the western world. As the churchmen of this time came to China by the same boats with the merchants and warriors, the Chinese people looked at them too with suspicious eyes. They were suspected of being aggressive imperialists and covetous capitalists in disguise, or of being at least tools. Moreover, the majority of the Chinese, converted to Christianity in the end of the Ching dynasty, did not belong to the families of the nobles and they even refused to participate in the Chinese traditional and sacrificial ceremonies. At last, the so-called Boxer's riot broke out and, for the first time in the history of China, the Chinese had religious persecution toward Christianity. To most Chinese, this riot is considered as a criminal act. Consequently, the rights of missionaries stipulated in the treaty were interpreted as punishment imposed upon China for the evacuation of the Allied Troops of the Eight Nations from Peking.

Twenty years later (or forty years ago) when the students of the Republic of China considered the penalty too severe, an anti-christian movement broke out again combined with an anti-imperialist and anti-capitalist movement. These movements led Chinese youth to believe materialistic Marxism and Leninism which are hostile to all religions and the Western world. But, if one has only a little knowledge of modern China, he will not be misled by the Communist occupation of Mainland China to conclude that the Chinese people are irreligious, materialistic by nature, or generally intolerant toward religions.

Outside of Mainland China, however, the influence of Christianity upon the Chinese is still advancing. There are many Chinese converted to Christianity with inner sincerity and deep devotion. But owing to the general poverty of the Chinese on one hand and western economical and political policies on the other hand, a Chinese after being converted to Christianity will usually get material benefits through Western churchmen. I cannot say, for sure, that Christianity is a religion deep-rooted in the culture and minds of the Chinese people.

A genuine Confucian may have a religious feeling of reverence for mystical union with Heaven or God through the realization of his moral nature which is directly conferred from Heaven. However, it is not necessary for him to be converted to any particular institutional religion. According to the doctrine of the sameness of humanity and the universality of Heaven, a genuine Confucian would believe that there is something common to all genuine religions, and that the differences among religions should be considered simply as different ways of attaining the same goal, and that one should pay reverence to all the sages of all religions. It is not necessary for us to judge which of the sages is the greatest and has attained the highest status of spirituality. Is it not more humble for us to suspend such judgment and keep silence on this question. concentrating our spiritual energy on admiring their greatness and cultivate our personalities toward attaining the stature they have already attained?

The only thing that can solve the dis-union and collision of different religions is neither religious syncretism nor religious imperialism, but a reverent attitude toward all genuine religions which are the different re-velations of the same Heaven or God or Brahma or Allah and at the same time different expressions of human religious spirit or human nature. This may be taken as a religious attitude to religions themselves which will bring the world of religions into a "great harmony" and transform all religious syncretism and imperialism.

In conclusion, we may quote a paragraph from the Doctrine of Mean which was supposed to have been written by a grandson of Confucius: "All things are nourished together without mutual injury. All the ways are parallel without collision. The smaller virtuous merits flow as rivers. The greater virtuous merits fulfill the transformation. It is this which makes Heaven and Earth so great."

This is the essence of Confucian thought, which is also more or less implied in Taoism and Chinese Buddhism, consciously or unconsciously expressed in the Chinese attitude toward world religions.

CHAPTER THREE

CHRISTIANITY

ROMAN CATHOLIC

CHARLES DONAHUE

Catholics and Non-Catholics

This statement of Roman Catholic principles and policies toward other faiths was written by a member of the Faculty of Fordham University, a Jesuit institution in New York City. Its primary aim was to correct the widespread opinion that Roman Catholics cannot believe that anyone outside the Catholic Church can be saved. It was published in 1957 by Harper and Brothers in the volume entitled, *Patterns of Faith in America Today*, pp. 118–120.

The Roman Catholic is necessarily an ecumenicist, a one-worlder. He is a member of a Church which he firmly holds is the Father's House, the spiritual home of all mankind. If the Catholic prays – and he does – that all mankind may be together in that House, he does not do so because he holds that all those not visibly and formally joined to the Church are in complete darkness, either religious or moral or intellectual. An "either/or" contrast between light within and darkness without is precisely such a harsh dichotomy as Catholic thinkers avoid. When the Catholic prays for unity, he prays that the light of those without may lead them to their home where, surely, their light will not be extinguished.

Consequently, while the Catholic is acutely conscious of the tragedy of religious disunity, Catholic doctrine holds forth the possibility of mitigating that tragedy somewhat through personal cooperation between Catholics and non-Catholics, between, let us say, the light within and the light without. Men, in Catholic doctrine, are brothers in a twofold fashion: supernaturally, since all are members, actual or potential, of the Mystical Body; naturally, since all are rational animals, the noblest beings of the material creation. An ecumenicism of nature is possible and worth striving for. We share all the natural things that bring men together; the arts and the sciences, all good social enterprises from the amenities of neighborhoods to the affairs of state. The Catholic should not act as though the Mystical Body were an in-group in the sociological sense, something to keep men apart in natural human concerns. That would be to misrepresent the spirit of the Church. And what is true of the unity of fellow citizens within a nation such as ours is equally true internationally. The tragic fact of world religious disunity is no excuse for standing cynically aside from efforts to bring international peace and well-being by natural means and by cooperation on a natural level.

But natural man, we have said, is a philosopher's abstraction. Interpersonal relationships, even though they may be concerned exclusively with natural things, necessarily have a supernatural, a religious, dimension. In his relationship with non-Catholic fellow citizens, neighbors, and friends, the Catholic is, of course, aware of this dimension. Agreement to disagree is the basis of any pluralist arrangement, and disagreement, even on the highest matters, need be no barrier to civic cooperation or deep friendship. Yet even cooperation and certainly friendship would be difficult if one party viewed the religious life of the other, the most profound stratum of his personality, with loathing and contempt. No such attitude toward religion outside the Church is suggested to the Catholic by Catholic doctrine. The Church teaches authoritatively that the incidence of God's grace is not confined to those within the Church. The supernatural life is, at least to a degree, open to all mankind. Catholic theologians hold that those who through no fault of their own cannot see the Church as Catholics see her may nevertheless lead valid religious lives by sincere following of the truth they do see. They are men of goodwill and their resolute pursuit of the good they see relates them in desire to the Church, a supernatural good which, though visible, they cannot see. The Catholic, therefore can only look with reverence on the religious lives of his non-Catholic friends and neighbors. They, too, are working out their I-Thou relationship with God. The Catholic sees their truth as uncompleted, but it is nonetheless truth, and he may often admire the zeal with which they live by it.

One could almost speak of an ecumenicism of goodwill, a supernatural fact, which unites with the ecumenicism of nature to mitigate the tragic fact of religious disunity. For the present, the ecumenicism of goodwill serves principally to make possible the sound personal fellowship necessary for cooperation on a natural level. Cooperation on a religious level, as for example, by participation in non-Catholic religious services is impossible for a Catholic. This does not mean, however, that the Catholic regards the prayers of non-Catholics as valueless. Protestants of goodwill who are pained by what they regard as our aloofness in this matter should consider that a Catholic who participated in a non-Catholic service would be violating his profoundest convictions on the Visible Church.

He would be enacting a lie and mocking his sincere Protestant friends with the simulacrum of a religious communion.[1]

Nevertheless the ecumenicism of goodwill can sometimes express itself on a religious level. As an archetype of the fruitful cooperation possible between branches of the Judeo-Christian tradition, I like to think of St. Thomas's respectful reading of Moses Maimonides and of the fruitfulness of that reading to St. Thomas's intellectual life as a Catholic. This kind of cooperation seems to be increasing today. Interested and equipped Catholics are reading Jewish and Protestant thinkers such as Buber, Barth, Tillich, and Niebuhr, and reading them with profit to their Catholicism. Jews and Protestants know the work of Maritain and Courtney Murray. They read papal statements with respect, often with admiration. On a more strictly personal level, there are Catholics – *experto crede* – who have been edified as Catholics by the character of Protestant and Jewish friends and enlightened as Catholics by their learning. I hope there have been cases where Catholics have been able to reciprocate.

Under our institutions, the least fruit one can expect from this activity is an increase of mutual empathetic understanding and consequently a more enthusiastic personal cooperation in all good natural works. The secatarian fierceness which harmed the cause of all religion is abating. This is happening without loss of intense religious conviction, without blurring of doctrinal differences at present irreconcilable, and without appeals to Caesar to give us a substitute for religion which will unite us. That is a considerable accomplishment. The rest can only be left to goodwill, prayer, and the grace of the God of Israel.

ANTONY ELENJIMITTAM, O.P.

A Christian Monk in a Hindu-Buddhist World

This statement by a Roman Catholic Dominican monk, of Indian nationality, is illustrative of the ways in which Indian Christians and Buddhists regard each other in their Hindu environment. It was first published in "World Mission", Vol. 8, Number 4, Winter 1957, pp. 96–101.

Non-Christians resent the very idea of setting the Christian Gospels at the top of everything. Protestant missionaries in India, specially J. N. Farquhar, have represented Christ as the Crown of Hinduism. To the

---

[1] I speak here of Protestants rather than of Protestants and Jews because, as far as I can judge from my own experience, Jews understand our attitude on this matter better than Protestants. Perhaps the reason for this is, in part, the fact that for Jews

newly emancipated nations of the colored continent any placing of white European culture and religion on top of their own national cultures is a matter for suspicion. The best way may be to present Jesus not as a transcendent crown, but as the very foundation and basis of a new evaluation of life. National cultures would be built on that new basis. The cultural superstructure, with its mansions and crown would then be leavened with the spirit of Christ, and we would find the unity of the Christian Gospel in a rich variety of national cultures. I read this meaning in the words of St. Paul:

"According to the grace of God that is given to me, as a wise architect, I have laid the foundation; and another buildeth thereon. But let every man take heed how he buildeth thereon. For other foundation no man can lay, but that which is laid, which is Christ Jesus." – I Cor. III, 10–11

It was one evening in October, 1949, that I reached the temple of Buddha Gaya, in the state of Bihar, in India. It is the most sacred pilgrimage spot for the entire Buddhist world, because there in Gaya, under the bo tree, Prince Siddharta became the Buddha, the Enlightened one of this age. Buddhist tradition ascribe this event to the full moon day in May, in the year 528 B. C. when Buddhha was in his thirty-fifth year. Emperor Asoka, after his conversion to Buddhism, resorted to that sacred spot for meditation and retreats. It was in the same place that Asoka, the greatest emperor of the greatest Indian empire, renounced everything and became a humble mendicant monk of Buddha. He sent his own brother Mahendra as a missionary to Ceylon, and from that place he inspired his own daughter Sangamitra, to become a Buddhist nun and go abroad for the spread of Buddhism in the third century B. C., when Buddhist missionary enterprise spread far beyond the confines of Asia.

I myself lived in a Buddhist monastery in Buddha Gaya with a view to studying that great religion and philosophy, not as a sceptic, a critic, nor as an apologist, but as a student and Christian missionary, with my mind and heart wide open to the religious and philosophical challenges of the Indian subcontinent. In Buddha Gaya, the Tibetans, the Burmese, the Chinese, and Ceylonese and other Buddhists have built their own monasteries where their monks and nuns stay. My very close association in those days with Bhikshu Jagadhise Kaysap, India's formeost Buddhist

as for Roman Catholics the visible and juridically organized community is an important religious fact. It is perhaps needless to add that Catholics may and sometimes do attend non-Catholic services where the circumstances make it clear that attendance does not imply participation.

philosopher and writer, and also an ideal monk, gave me entrance to the *sancta sanctorum* of all the Buddhist monasteries in Buddha Gaya, Gaya Kalimpong and many other places in India.

Dressed in saffron robes and carrying my mendicant's begging bowl, I toured many of the interior villages of Bihar with my Buddhist friend. In my bag I carried a copy of the Bhagavad Gita, the Upanishads, selections from other religious scriptures, and the Buddhist Dhammapada. In the beginning I faced the Hindu-Buddhist public under the sheltering wings of my Buddhist monk, Bhikshu Kaysap. His love of Lady Poverty, his chastity and his lofty ideals had all endeared him to me. Kaysap, in his turn imagined that I was following in the footsteps of St. Francis of Assisi in my life, and of St. Thomas Aquinas in my intellectual pursuits.

Both of us felt mutually enriched through the exchange of experiences, ideals and spiritual treasures. What a world of difference it makes to learn religion and philosophy from books and journals on the one hand and from a living soul whose mind and heart derive their nourishment, enlightenment and apostolic zeal from a deep religious faith! How true is the Indian concept that the deeper religious truths are never acquired from books but directly, either from God or from God-guided masters and self-realized *gurus* (teachers).

As a Dominican and an Indian, the ideal of a mendicant monk engaged in itinerant preaching was, and still is, my vocation. Soon my Buddhist comrade, Bhikshu Kaysap had to go to the Benares Hindu University where he was teaching Buddhism and Pali literature. This meant that the nestling now had to come out and fly without the protection of the mother-bird. A fair amount of knowledge of the Hindu scriptures in their original Sanskrit, and of the Buddhist scriptures in both Hindu translation and in Pali, and an ability to express my ideas in Hindi or Urdu gave me the confidence to face any Hindu or Buddhist audience.

Usually a little after dawn and also about half-and-hour before the sunset was the time I found most suitable to sit down for religious discussions and prayermeetings. There was no need of a bell or signs for calling. It was enough for me to go and squat under a tree, clad in saffron robes and with my religious books, for people to come uninvited. If the audience were purely Hindu, I would begin my prayer meeting with the singing of Gayatri, or with readings from the Bhagavad Gita or the Upanishads in Sanscrit, with its Hindu translation and commentary. The people are ready to hear you if you have entered through their own door. Once their confidence had been gained, it was not difficult for me to open my Bible especially the New Testament and read passages from it explaining as I went along. I would show them texts and ideas which were paralleled in Indian Traditions but stressing the specific and unique contributions Jesus Christ and His Gospel and His Church could make to the new life of Independent India.

For months on end, I toured from village to village, always sticking to the same routine, viz., prayer meetings in the mornings for the Hindu-Buddhist public, and open discussion-forums in the evenings, always beginning with the Hindu-Buddhist scriptures and philosophies and terminating with the Christian Gospel. This does not simply mean entering through their door and coming out through ours. It requires humility and psychology to sit on the last step of the ladder; and yet to be sure of one's specific faith and of superiority on the part of Christian missionaries is self-destructive, in the changed socio-political set-up of India and the Asian Continent.

Most educated Hindus have nothing but admiration, love and appreciation for the Gospel of Jesus Christ. Even the illiterate Hindu has an instinctive reverence for the person of Jesus, and also for His Church. Only the Hindu who has studied in the West or has lived for a long time in Europe feels indifferent, or even hostile, to any attempt to depict the Church as the only ark of salvation. Western education as received in the West is, for the most part, likely to prejudice colored students against Christianity of any denomination. Race-consciousness and a lingering pride in native culture and religion are often very serious obstacles which prevent them from embracing Christianity in its entirety.

Indians, generally speaking, have little historic sense. Their religions and philosophies are rooted in the timeless vision of the Absolute at whose tabernacle little respect is paid to the time-space-bound world or to historicity and a well-organized Church. Christ without the Church is more acceptable to the Indian people than the Church, with or without Christ.

I remember a group of university students from Patna inviting me to address them on comparative religion. At the end of the discussion that followed my talk, a certain Bengali boy came to me and said: "We want Christ as the heart of our being, but not as the whole of our being." I asked him: "What do you mean by that?" He replied: "In philosophic speculation our brains cannot be beaten by the so-called Christian West. We shall not budge an inch from our cultural soul. We shall leave the doors and windows of our soul wide open to any new light that comes not only from Christianity but from any side; but we shall not be swept off from our feet. Jesus is one of ours; He is an Asian. We understand

Him better than the Europeans. Why should we accept their versions which, usually, displace our cultural soul? So I will say, let Christ remain in our hearts, with His religion of love of God above everything and of neighbour as ourselves; but we should not be Christians who become like the westeners in everything except in the color of our skins." This is the general attitude among most of the educated Hindus. We have to accept this fact, not only in the lives of great modern Indians like Mahatma Gandhi, Rabindranath Tagore, Sarvepalli Radhakrishnan and others, but also in the mentality of an average educated Indian nationalist. Acceptance of this fact enables us to be realists, not simply brushing aside the facts of race-psychology and national consciousness. It is not enough to say that the Hindus believe that all religions are the same, and that therefore there is no need, or hope of conversions. This platitude of equality of religions, when examined more closely will be found to consist in the following statement: All religions have different degrees of truth in them; but not all religions are true. To an enquiring mind, nothing is true because it is ours. We cannot say: "This is ours and so it must be true." On the contrary we should say: "This is truth and so it is ours."

We, as ambassadors of Christ and missionaries of the Catholic Church, must have the courage to face Truth, from whatever angle it may shine. The presence of the Hindu-Buddhist world is a real and great challenge to Christian values, not only in the universities and intellectual centers of the West, but even more in the field of the missionary apostolate in the East. We cannot shrink from the issue nor side-step the challenge of the cultural and spiritual heritage of the newly independent nations of Asia. Hindu-Buddhist faith and ideology give today spiritual nourishment to over one third of mankind. To win the confidence and trust of this vast Asian continent is now essential for any fruitful intellectual apostolate in India, or for any other Asian country. We can inspire confidence in them only by sincere and genuine acceptance of all that is true and sublime, in their religious traditions, their philosophy, their art and their history. Our watchword should be acceptance, not rejection; assimilation, not ostracism; humble and loving service, not arrogant superiority.

I have been asked: "What on earth have you gained by donning Hindu robes, by quoting Sanscrit scriptures and preaching Buddhism? Have you baptized your hearers? You have thereby only confirmed (them) in their own beliefs and weakened the Christian position." My reply to my critics in those days was: "Christ did not send me only to baptize but to preach; setting an example, as best as I may, to the flock. I must be a Hindu to

my Hindu fellow-countrymen, a Buddhist to my fellow-Asiatics, in order
to lead them to the basic teachings of Jesus, not by rejecting their own
cultural moorings, but by impregnating their culture with the spirit of
Jesus and Him Crucified. The number of non-Christians I have baptized
is to be counted on my fingers: but those to whom I have brought the
Gospel of Jesus are to be counted by several hundreds of thousands. As
an Indian Dominican missionary priest this is my God-given vocation,
and I must be true to it, as the others must abound and grow in the gifts
and lights they have received from God.

EASTERN ORTHODOX

SERGE VERHOSKOY

The Relationship of the Eastern Orthodox Church to Other Churches

The author is the Rev. Professor of Dogmatic Theology at St. Vladimir's
Orthodox Catholic Seminary Academy in New York City. Though the
Eastern Churches are less integrated than the Roman Catholic Church,
this statement represents a point of view generally recognized as authoritative among all Eastern Orthodox Churches.

The relationship of the Eastern Orthodox Church to other Churches
is governed by three principles: (1) that the fullness of the religious life is
possible only in Christ; (2) that communion with Christ is possible only
in the Church; and (3) that the Church must possess the infallible knowledge of truth.

If the goal of religious life is the restoration of the perfectness of
humanity and a complete communion with God, then the fulfilment of
the goal is possible only in Christ, the God-Man, who by His life, death,
and resurrection transformed humanity in Himself and laid the foundation
of the Kingdom of God and the future transformation of the world.
Christ, as perfect God and perfect Man, united in one Person, unites the
whole of mankind, indeed the whole of creation, with the Deity. But the
perfect union of the Deity with humanity must be mutual. This is made
possible through the Church, which is the unity of all those united with
Christ and through Him with God. To be in the Church means to be in
Christ, and conversely, to be outside the Church means to be outside
Christ, and consequently outside the fullness of the divine-human unity.
To be only a nominal Christian is not enough. One must have the true
Faith and the grace of God which a Christian may receive through the

Sacraments and the endeavors of his whole life. This is why the Eastern Orthodox Church does not presuppose the attainment of this fullness of life by those who are not members, nor does it affirm that the formal or nominal belonging to the Christian community is enough for eternal salvation. Such an affirmation would clearly be in contradiction with the Scriptures and with the Church's own inner historical experience.

From the Scriptural texts and from the teachings of Orthodox theologians, it is possible to conclude that all those who do not belong to the Eastern Orthodox Church are destined for eternal damnation. However, such a conclusion would be a gross exaggeration. It is clear that God, being perfectly just and perfectly merciful, does not permit damnation to come to those who have not committed some act worthy of damnation, or who have failed to take care of their salvation solely because of ignorance and through no fault of their own. It would then follow and seem logical that those who are outside the Church because they really do not know of her as she is, cannot be deserving of damnation. However, so far as the Church is concerned, the fate of those outside her is the complete mystery of God's Providence. One cannot deny that even outside the Church the knowledge of certain fundamental truths is possible (for example, the existence of God, some basic principles of morality, a desire for eternal salvation, a knowledge of divine-human encounter, etc.) Such knowledge can bring those outside the Church closer to the true life, even if it is only partial.

Truly Christian relationships with other confessions and religions can only be relationships of love and effort to convert them by preaching and examples of good deeds. The one desire of the Orthodox Church must be to make the entire world Orthodox, bringing all people together in unity with Christ. This is not religious imperialism but simple logic as humanity cannot be saved without the unity with God in the fullness of Truth. The Truth and the possibilities of a perfect life were given to the Church by God and not created by the Church, therefore, if we believe in the necessity of the Church for salvation, it is not because of our own merits.

The Eastern Church has often been persecuted by other religions. The Orthodox people at times have been forced to defend their Faith by the use of arms. If it is true that the governments of certain countries, whose populations are predominantly Orthodox, have persecuted and constricted other religions, the Church, as such, never approved of the use of force against other believers. In general, the relationship of the Eastern Orthodox Church to other religions has been rather peaceful, particularly when the latter have not persecuted Orthodoxy.

ANGLICAN

WILLIAM TEMPLE

The Case for Evangelization

This is an excerpt from the Proceedings of *The Jerusalem Meeting of the International Missionary Council* (1928) Vol. I. pp. 368–379). The author, at the time Bishop-Designate of York, later Archbishop of Canterbury, made this analysis of the relation of the Christian religion to others in the context of the Council's discussion of "secularism." It remains an important formulation of the Anglican point of view.

The comparative study of religion has commonly been pursued by those who had little or no personal conviction of the uniqueness of the Christian revelation. Consequently it has tended to start with the assumption that all religions stand, more or less, on a level; they are treated as variants of one general tendency of the human mind; if there is any divine impulse behind them it is sought chiefly in that general tendency rather than in the distinctive features of any particular religion; and so far as it is allowed that one religion has more divine authority than another, this is understood to mean that it corresponds better with the real nature of the impulse that finds expression in all religions.

But to begin thus is to begin with the unproved denial of the claim which Christianity makes. It is not to be wondered at that, having made this great assumption, the comparative study of religion goes on to trace parallels and resemblances in every direction; nor that, having traced these, it should create in the popular mind a belief that the inner essence of all religions is identical while they differ in the vehicles of their expression. They differ widely and deeply in their essence, for the essence of a religion is the character of the God to whom worship is offered...

Now the comparative study of religion has been conducted on anthropological and psychological lines. To pursue it upon those lines has been perfectly legitimate, so long as the limitations involved were recognized. All religions have aspects for which such study is appropriate. But no religion, in the estimate of its own adherents, is exhausted by those aspects. Every religion maintains that it is not only a state of mind in those who practice it, but an apprehension of a Truth which is independent of their minds altogether; and its whole significance for them resides in this. Consequently the process by which the comparative study of religions has appeared to put all religions on a level is one which first eviscerates all religions of all that causes anyone to care about them. In other words, if what this sort of comparative study can tell us were the whole truth, there would be no religions at all to be studied or compared.

The essential element in any religion is its claim to be true, whether partially and relatively, or completely and absolutely; to put it another way, the essential element in any religion is not to be found in a human attitude toward something, but in the something towards which that human attitude is assumed. The essential element in any religion is the character of its God, and it is here that religions deeply differ from one another...

For how are we to proceed from the assertion of the uniqueness of Christ to its demonstration, unless there is instituted a comparison between the Gospel and other religions at their best? Moreover, uniqueness is not the only attribute of the Gospel; universality is another. And how are we to present Christ as the fulfilment, and more than the fulfilment, of the highest aspirations of the many races of mankind, unless we know sympathetically what those highest aspirations are?...

We maintain that Jesus Christ is more than one among many divinely inspired teachers; we maintain that He is actually God. And we make this claim for Him, not chiefly in order to honor the historical Jesus; He sought no such honor. We make this claim for Him because what is of vital consequence is the character of God. It is not because He had a new conception of God that men have found in Jesus Christ the Savior of themselves and of the world; it is because they have found Him to be Himself the Eternal God.

This claim can be finally established only by a complete philosophy and the experience of mankind. But it glows as a conviction of faith at the very heart of Christianity. We do not expect to see it logically proved; what we have a right to expect is that when applied to actual problems, practical or theoretical, it should guide us towards a solution; and this is what we actually find. Yet it is not the strength of its intellectual position by which it wins victories over individuals or races: it is its manifest power to re-create alike the soul and society. "As many as received Him, to them gave He the right to become children of God." (John I : 12) That is not the utterance of an aspiration: it is the record of an observed fact, and it is the observation of that fact that has drawn, and still draws men to Christ as the source of the new vitalizing power...

To the Christian there should be no need to argue the case for evangelization; yet it seems that it is necessary, for Christians often fail to apprehend the nature of their own religion. They think of it as one among the religions of mankind, and look out for its distinctive characteristics, and contendedly classify themselves as Christians, and others as Muslims, or Hindus, or whatever it may be, as though they were speaking of so many political parties. They think of Christianity as the appropriate religion for Europeans or Americans, while Islam is the appropriate religion for Arabs and Hinduism for Indians. But Christianity is not just one phase of human opinion. Its whole significance depends upon its claim to be absolute and final. If that quality is denied to it, it sinks at once to the level of any human speculation or aspiration, and ceases to be the faith for which the martyrs have died.

There is nothing in this claim hostile to that belief in perpetual development which is so dear to the mind of the present generation. That for which finality is claimed is not a system of thought or a code of ethics: it is a personal life. In the understanding of that life and in the application of its spirit and principles to every kind of problem there is room for strictly endless development. But if Christ was and is what Christians believe Him to be, it certainly follows that there can be no future revelation by which He could possibly be superseded; in just the same way the multiplication table cannot be superseded, but this is not regarded as a hindrance to the development of mathematical science.

But while this claim to finality leaves ample room for progress and development, it leaves none, as the multiplication table leaves none, for any notion that it may be the right belief for some and not for others. The Gospel is not first and foremost a medicine to heal ourselves, adapted to some maladies and not to others. It is first and foremost, Truth, and is efficacious as medicine for men's souls only in proportion as it is accepted as Truth. And if it is Truth, then very plainly it is the Truth which is most important for men to know. It is because it is the Truth and in it reality is expressed that to conform to it is to build one's house upon the rock...

It is a plain fact of history that the great advance of Natural Science has taken place in Christendom and not outside it. It may be rash to argue, as some students of the subject have done, that science is itself a fruit of Christianity, but it may be safely asserted that it can never spontaneously grow up in regions where the ruling principle of the Universe is believed to be either capricious or hostile, and when it is imported into those regions it is bound to undermine such a belief. There is a kinship between the scientific impulse and the essential elements in Christianity which explains how science could win its triumphs in Christendom and at least inspires a hope that it will not destroy but strengthen Christian faith.

But the first impact of Natural Science upon a civilization is liable to result in materialism. The immensely increased control over nature makes men feel independent of any higher power, and the concentration on material goods and the processes of producing them and distributing them diverts attention from spiritual interests. Now this urgent materialism of a scientific civilization is too powerful to be merely repressed; it may be controlled or sublimated (as the current jargon has it) but not repressed. And it cannot be controlled by any religion which either is immersed in the material or turns its back upon it. What is the Hindu reformer to do with steam and electricity? His religion says they are part of the illusion of life; it will not help him to control them. He may try to neglect them, as Mr. Gandhi does, but they will be too strong for him. Or he may keep his religion in one compartment and his political or social action in another; and then the compartment allocated to religion will shrink while the other expands. What is wanted is a religion for which matter is the proper vehicle of spirit, and spirit is recognized to act by directing matter; and Christianity alone answers to that description. Its central affirmation is that "the Word was made flesh." It is the most materialistic of all higher religions, for while they attain to spirituality by turning away from matter, it expresses its spirituality by dominating matter. After all, the only purely spiritual things in the world are good intentions; and we all know where that road leads which is paved by them. For Christianity, matter exists to be the vehicle of spirit, and is only fulfilling its true function when it is that; but spirit realizes itself by controlling matter and only expresses itself so far as it does that. Taught by the Incarnation, the Christian finds all the universe a sacrament, which finds its focal expression in the Word made flesh.

This carries with it the obligations not only of personal selfcontrol but of subduing the whole material order of society to the Spirit of Christ. To make what is now the sphere of ruthless competition an expression of true fellowship is the great need of the whole civilized world. That aspiration so entirely coheres with the Christian Gospel as to be almost part of it. Here too the Gospel gives us the direction in which progress must be made.

Yet one more, the political discovery of the modern world is democracy, and the moral root of democracy is respect for individual personality. But the very notion of personality as we conceive it today is a product of Christianity. Democracy is a child of the Gospel. And it desperately needs the Gospel to keep it wholesome; for it is liable to two perversions. One of these is that chaotic license for which Plato denounces democracy. If the true principle that all personality is sacred is held without regard to the balancing principle that we are all members one of another, it leads to moral and social chaos; in Christianity these two principles are held in even balance. But modern democracy is still more likely to suffer from the other perversion. Its inevitable machinery of majorities and mass meetings tends to give a most unwholesome development to the herd instinct; thus the majority becomes tyrannous, and individuality is crushed. The only sound reason for giving authority to a majority is that this is the only way to give full weight to the personal quality in every citizen; therefore the right of the majority to govern is inseparable from the right of the minority to hold its own convictions; and democracy is true to itself only when it has the most delicate sensitiveness of conscience about the rights of minorities. It is under perpetual temptation to trample on them; only if its spiritual roots – belief in human brotherhood under God's Fatherhood – are strong, is there any hope of its resisting them. What we need is independence of thought and the spirit of fellowship; what modern urbanized civilization is creating is herd-mentality with a spirit of pugnacity. This perversion will be cured only by a power more compelling than the influence of social environment – by a religion, therefore. But it must be a religion in which the root principle of democracy is strong.

PROTESTANT

R. PIERCE BEAVER

*Mutual Understanding and Study among Religions
From the Viewpoint of the Christian Mission*

The author is Professor of Missions in the Federated Theological Faculty of the University of Chicago. In 1957, he visited the headquarters of the Ramakrishna Mission in Calcutta, India. His lecture on this occasion (published in the *Bulletin of the Ramakrishna Mission Institute of Culture*, Oct. 1957, pp. 229–236) together with the discussion that followed it, was a notable instance of two active missionary bodies confronting each other frankly and amiably. The following extracts from this lecture give the essential "viewpoint of the Christian mission" as interpreted by Professor Beaver. The viewpoint of the Ramakrishna Mission is presented under *"Hinduism"*.

World-wide missionary activity on the part of so many religions unavoidably brings their adherents into intimate contact. When such confrontation occurs, four attitudes are possible. There may be hostility, mutual attack and recrimination; and unfortunately there are devotees of each of the faiths who unmercifully and unfairly attack the others. It would be tragic if the missionary efforts of the various religions would result in bitter antagonism at a time when the world needs spiritual illumination for the healing of its brokenness. A "holy war" of words would be about as bad as a "holy war" of the sword. Another possible attitude would be mutual recognition of each other's right to witness to and propagate its faith, non-interference in each other's affairs, and frigid politeness in passing. Two other attitudes might be that of mutual exchange in friendly and serious conversations, and positive cooperation. At the present stage, it is not likely that there will be much of the latter. There has been little cooperation excepting for the success which the Ramakrishna Mission and the Unitarians have each achieved in drawing together the representatives of many faiths. In a more limited field there has been an active fellowship of Catholics, Protestants and Jews in the United States. At present, we sorely need mutual understanding and respect. Conversations and common study of major spiritual issues, such as the nature and destiny of man, would be highly desirable. They would help to prevent religious controversy, build bridges of friendship, provide each faith a chance to witness to its understanding of truth, and bring to all a more profound understanding of the divine will for mankind...

Some attention was given to the subject at the Second Assembly of the World Council of Churches at Evanston in 1954, and subsequently a Consultation on Christianity and the Other Religions was held at Davos, Switzerland, in July, 1955, under the joint sponsorship of the Department of Evangelism of the World Council of Churches and the Department of Missionary Studies of the W.C.C. and International Missionary Council. Out of that consultation has come a long term study programme, which is just now getting under way. It will involve group study and discussion and also stimulate individual effort.

Perhaps the three important things which came out of the Davos Consultation were these: Christianity as a system is not to meet other religions as systems, but Christians are to meet persons who are adherents of other religious systems; the Christian's task in that meeting is not to oppose other systems and views, but to introduce Jesus Christ as the Friend of every man; and the study is to be taken up at a point beyond the Kraemer-Hocking debate.

As Christians, engaged in a world-wide mission, look forward to conversations with earnest followers of other faiths, there is a genuine appreciation of many aspects of those faiths, but at the same time, on the part of most, a fear of syncretism. Fresh, new insights into this difficult issue of relationship are needed to guide Christians in their efforts to understand and appreciate the living faiths of others. At the same time, many Christians are coming to the conviction that the chief function of the Church is the proclamation that God is in Christ reconciling the world unto Himself, and they are wishing to make that testimony in friendship and through conversations.

This, then, is in brief the state of mind with respect to other religions which one finds today in the cooperating Protestant missions. I sincerely hope that this survey has been of some value in contributing to better understanding in this day when the need of the world so urgently calls all seekers for truth to a common study and conversation to the end that we may know better the divine will for man and may act in unison for the establishment of a just, righteous and brotherly world order.

PADIPEDDI CHENCHIAH

Christianity and Non-Christian Faiths

This statement by the Chief Judge of Pudukkottai State, and leading Christian layman in India is taken from a from a group of essays submitted by members of the *Christo Samaj* to the Tambaram (Madras) World Missionary Conference of 1938. The Appendix of the volume, "Rethinking Christianity in India," Madras, 1939 is devoted to a criticism of Hendrik Kraemer's *The Christian Message in a Non-Christian World,* and it is from this Appendix (pp. 19 ff) that the following statement is taken.

The present context of history demands urgently that we should rediscover Jesus in the light of our colossal needs. The enquiry bears intimately on the purpose of incarnation and the unveiling of new powers imperatively needed by us in our conflicts in society and State. Today we have to realize Jesus as the head of a new world order; or as the creative expression of God's higher purposes with regard to man. On all these topics we seek in vain for enlightenment. The Christianity we seek to compare not being in itself clear to us, our comparison suffers in clarity and the findings reached are bound to be devoid of any permanent value. The comparison of Christianity as we know it, with non-Christian faiths as we construe them to be, does not yield true differentia. Nor can we compare with any profit the unknown features and factors in Jesus with the unexplored potentialities of non-Christian faiths. The supreme gain of comparative study, better still, of the co-living of faiths, is the light they throw on each other and the new phases they disclose. We start to compare and we find that the things to be compared have changed in the process...

Whatever value the transcendence of God might have, one fails to see any justification for the transcendence of Jesus. The primary error which deflected the true current of thought as to Jesus began when we set him along with God over against man and made him exclusively the object of worship. This, one cannot help feeling, is a total distortion of the purpose, of the meaning and message of Jesus, though arising out of devotion and piety. The Incarnation has its spearhead toward creation. To turn it round and make it face heaven is to reverse its purpose. Confusion is due to the use of the word incarnation- an unbiblical term. In the company of Jesus we do not feel the gulf that separates God from man. We feel he is the bridge, the hyphen that unites God and man. His own consciousness reveals the total lack of this sense of separation and his teachings do not emphasize the awful gulf between God and man. Else, our Lord would not have bid us to be perfect like God. The desire to be like God was the sin of Adam but the virtue of the Christian. The emphasis on 'the Son' in the 'Son of God' and 'Son of Man' is illuminating. Jesus is not God and is not Man, but is the Son of God and the Son of Man. The word 'Son' indicates the measure of unity – something less than complete identity with God but something more than difference in category – between God, Jesus, and the Christian. God is God. Man is Man. The twain have met in Jesus: not merely met, but fused and mingled into one. Hinduism always longed for a state in which we could say as Jesus did, 'I and my Father are one' – which was our Lord's affirmation of the Brahma Vakya *Aham Brahmasmi*. It may be, in the mouth of a mere man, the assertion is a travesty. In Jesus it was, for the first time in history an accomplished reality, not an unrealised aspiration. India will not be afraid of claiming Jesus as belonging to our race as the head of humanity, as the Son of Man. This is the message of Christianity that the Word has become flesh and God has become man....

There is an aspect of the Sermon on the Mount which is a summation of the basic principles of human life. The Western is impressed with the unfamiliarity of the Sermon on the Mount to his accustomed mode of action, but to the Indian they appear to be familiar. I do not suggest that the Hindu is prone to love his enemy cheerfully or naturally, but not having been used to demand an eye for an eye or tooth for a tooth, the counsel does not appear to be unnatural or extravagant.

It is well known that the intelligentsia in India are profoundly affected by two streams of Russian thought – one reaching India through Tolstoy and the Mahatma, forming the foundation of a new social outlook which builds national life on love and non-violence and the other reaching us through Jawaharlal Nehru intimately connected with the social reconstruction of national life on communistic doctrines. Mahatma Gandhi's attempt is to detach the Christian principles from the personality of Jesus and make them instruments of social and political reconstruction. This attempt has a good and worthy tradition. Christian ethics first impressed Raja Ram Mohan Roy and since his days it has been acting as a social ferment, starting a long train of reforms within Hinduism. But the ethical influence of Christianity never reached anything like a wide scale operation nor was regarded as a definite principle of construction instead of criticism, till Mahatma made his first experiments with it in South Africa. The Christian Church in India has been following this movement with hope, joy and fervent prayer as the first application of Christian principles to units larger than the individual....

What is it you are going to preach to the Hindu and for what purpose are we going to ask him to renounce his faith? For the pursuit of the chimera of the absolute? For chasing after a Kingdom of God which can never be realised? For aspiring after a Jesus who though born as we are of a human mother can never be attained by us? Is it not an irony that after beating the big drum of the superior claims of Christianity, to anounce a religion too absolute to be realised in this relative world? Realisation has been the heart and soul of the Indian view of spiritual life. Are we to preach the supreme Gospel of the non-realisability of God and Jesus?...

Apart from the Sermon on the Mount and a few sayings of the Lord, we cannot get any guidance for our social and political problems from reading the Bible. We cannot by imitating Jesus get the necessary enlightenment for the problems of our day. God does not speak to us as He did in the days of the prophet. We have no ready access to Him and He does not answer our questions. We have lost faith in witches, necromancers, mediums who pretend to know the will of God. What then is the use of this empty boast that ours is a theocentric ethics depending entirely on the knowledge of the will of God? What appeal can this impracticable claim make on the Hindus? We cannot expect them to take the Church at her own valuation. They are, whatever they may not be, a shrewd lot. They can see through us and our pretensions. The truth of the matter seems to be that we are bound to be caught in this vicious circle so long as we regard Christian ethics as the external standard of conduct... In the new life after rebirth there are no internal conflicts or external demands but merely spontaneous outflow of action. We love our enemies not against the grain of our nature nor from obedience to the extraneous will of God but because that happens to be the natural expression of the new life. The secret of Christian ethic does not arise from any new mode of appreciation or insight but from new creative life which is the first and last distinction between Christianity and other religions...

If we take the 'revelation' claimed in different religions, we have to confess that they do not piece together or form an intelligible whole. The Vedas, the Koran, the Gospel do not make a coherent scheme. They do not even answer the same question. An impartial student is moved to a healthy scepticism of revelation and to entertain doubts whether God reveals, apart from creation and whether true revelation is not a creative act. Revelation is not knowledge inaccessible to man. There is precious little of that type of knowledge in the so-called revelations. God's dealings in various religions have been negatively to give 'salvation' in the sense of redemption from sin or positively to draw out the potentiality in man. If we do not recognise this or if you maintain that this has occurred only in Christianity, we wander in the wilderness...

The prevailing view among the orthodox missionaries of an earlier generation was that non-Christian religions are a vast decaying degrading section of the spiritual life of mankind. There are various grades in this belief which it is unnecessary to examine... It was born in ignorance and bigotry and cannot survive the light of knowledge. Nor can we grade religions, according to Christianity the highest place. Every religion is a circle complete and perfect in itself. Though not consciously, yet in fact, they start with a quest which they more or less achieve. Religions are really incomparable. At any rate, we have no principle, reasonable and acceptable, which can be applied to evolve a calculus of religions.

The theory that all religions are substantially the same and are roads leading to the same goal though held by some of the most intellectual of religious leaders in India, has to be taken more as a token of goodwill and a hope for brotherliness of religions, than as a serious proposition, capable of any proof. Religions must have a common basis, just as all men must have a skeleton. But that does not constitute the equality of men, nor account for all the richness and variety which constitutes life...

One important aspect of the problem is often overlooked. In all religions there is a residue of unfulfilled desire, partly arising out of the very satisfaction religion achieves and partly out of the failure of religion to satisfy the aspirations of man so far. Jesus stands in definite relation to the residuary problems of other religions rather than with the satisfied longings of man. In other words, the relationship of Christ to the non-Christian heart and hope lies in the unexplored regions of our Lord's life and not in the region already mapped out. Here the doctrine of fulfilment has some bearing...

The Church and Christian society in the West are in a turmoil. On the field, the prestige of the West as invaders or purveyors of a superior culture, has fast declined. Non-Christian faiths are taking a new life, vivified by a dynamic of nationalism. While Christian ideals may likely spread quickly in Eastern lands, conversions in the sense of annexations to the Church or society may be opposed not only by society but also by the State. Hinduism challenged by the crisis of the times manages to put forth unprecedented vigour in the moral sphere and the State by apt legislation is removing disabilities that acted as the best recruiting agent for Islam and Christianity. For one thing the missionary has to rely entirely on the spiritual resources of Christianity and not on the material resources of his own country nor on the adverse social conditions of the depressed. The urge to spread the Gospel is perennial in Christianity. If old methods and forces serve us no longer, new powers should be discovered, new weapons forged.

In the past, evangelism was conceived as a warfare. Christian and non-Christian faiths were ranged as enemeies with their weapons, mostly disputation, turned against each other. The missionary and his sharp-shooters ventured periodically into the enemy's territory, gave engagements and returned occasionally with captives of war. This was the atmosphere in which St. Paul not infrequently preached the Gospel. But this need not be the perpetual atmosphere of religions. Among religions, the spirit of bellicose hostility must cease. The Hindu should not feel that the moment he nods, the enemy will snatch away some of his fold. We must live as friends and love each other and in that atmosphere spread the Gospel...

If Christianity is to permeate Hindu Society, the whole policy, aim and methods have to be changed. In the new programme, speaking tentatively, the following lines of work may be developed:

1. The policy of individual or mass conversion with the avowed object of forming the converts into a community or a Church should be abandoned.

2. The idea that a person should be either a Hindu or a Christian should also be relinquished. This may work all right for statistical purposes, but is not according to the process of life, which does not operate by

clear cut distinctions. In India we must be prepared to see the gradual infusion of Hinduism by Christian ideals and above all Christian life. We must force the pace of this process.

3. We may with profit learn a lesson – a valuable one, from the way in which Western Culture has succeeded in making headway in the East. This way consists in creating an atmosphere rather than a solid nucleus, whether a community or a Church. To create a powerful Christian atmosphere within Hinduism appears to be the immediate task.

4. The successful working out of this line of approach first requires a mental change which permits us to look on life as energy and power and not as numbers. We must conceive the function whether of the Church or of community not in terms of expansion but in terms of movements created within Hinduism changing its outlook into that of Christ.

Before we formulate an evangelical programme for the Indian Church, we must study the psychology of the Indian mind. We have to discover along what tracks, mental and moral energy spreads in Hindu society. In the East personality exercises more influence than institution. You must have a seer or rishi before you can open the mind of a Hindu. In this connection there is room for research work....

Right in the heart of Hinduism, there has always been a conception of religion which means a widening, deepening or enlarging of human personality – a problem different from education – the working out of potentialities. All this spiritual effort, intensely personal, went by the names of Yoga. The Buddhist, Hindu Vedist, and Bhakta all agreed on this point. It represented a discipline above the ethical. It concerned personality and the roots of our being. Till the Christian discovers or discloses the Christian Yoga of rebirth, we skirmish on the outskirts. Here is the fundamental weakness of the Church. Rebirth has become a doctrine, else toned down into repentance for the simple reason that the Holy Spirit has become a doctrine or sanctified reason. Unless we conceive of this new birth as a biological process, a process which like life covers the physical, mental, and moral, we miss its significance. India awaits the fruition of this experiment. It is on the tiptoe of expectation. Already some of the mature souls of modern India have caught the fascination of the great experiment.

It is all a question who discovers first. He will be the great evangelist. Church and Baptism, names, are all labels. We need to possess reality. India has always searched for reality and yielded to reality. The future of Christianity lies in the spiritual laboratory. The Indian Christian must concern himself with 'rebirth'. God gave Jesus. True evangelism consists in reproducing Jesus. The process is Christianity. When we have discovered it, the Hindu will besiege you, instead of your begging for his attention. Let the foreign missionary preach and teach. Let the professional organs of the Church plan campaigns, join battles. The Indian Christian who can see deeper should take to the prayer room and experiment on *rebirth*, – harness the Holy Spirit to the creation of new life.

CHAPTER FOUR

HINDUISM

SWAMI SANKARANANDA

The Attitude of Hinduism toward non-Hindu Religions

Swami Sankarananda is President of Ramakrishna Math and Mission, Belur Math (Howrah), West Bengal, India, which is the Mission's Headquarters.

To a casual observer, Hinduism looks like a multitude of faiths and sects, some of which are apparently contradictory. But when one dives deep into its spiritual depths, one realizes the principle at the back of these various and sometimes apparently contradictory faiths and sects. Behind Hindu civilization for the last five thousand years or more, there has been a certain inspiring universal ideal which has fashioned its course. This principle is still alive and dynamic.

In ancient civilizations we find there were tribal gods, and there was fight for the supremacy of one or other of these. In India, too, in the early Vedic age, there were various gods struggling for supremacy; but fortunately for Hinduism, one great sage solved this conflict by enunciating a great principle, "Truth is one, sages call it by various names." (Rig Veda) The whole history of Hindu civilisation is influenced by this thought. Time and again, great Prophets, Incarnations and saints have come in this land reiterating this central doctrine, which has thereby gained in force during these thousands of years. The one great truth, therefore, for which Hinduism stands, is not merely toleration, but acceptance of all faiths. "As different rivers, taking their start in different mountains and flowing through different lands, finally come to the same ocean, even so the different faiths that men embrace because of different temperaments finally lead to Thee" – so sings a Hindu sage. (Mundaka Upanishad) The Hindu believes that every worship under whatever name or form is offered to Him, the Truth.

The Hindus believe in the Vedas. The Vedas are not mere books, but the record of certain fundamental spiritual laws or truths like the immanence of God and divinity of the soul, discovered by great sages, even as scientific laws or truths are discovered in the material world by scientists. These laws were already working in nature and were only discovered by the scientists. So also these spiritual laws were there from the beginning of time for they are eternal truths and were only discovered by the sages and recorded in the Vedas. The proof of these spiritual truths is direct realization by every one in the super-conscious state; they do not depend on the sanction of any prophet, however great. This realization of God or the eternal truths is not limited bij time, space or race, but is the birthright of every person. Prophets and Incarnations are but illustrations of these eternal truths. They work out the details according to time, place, racial temperaments and needs, so that man can easily attain the Truth.

To the Hindus, the expression, 'I am the way' really means that the life and teachings of Christ are a way of God-realization. It is the firm conviction of the Hindus that no single religion can suit all men, for all of them are not of the same temperament, and in order that everyone may have a religion suited to him, there should be many religions, which will allow everyone to have a religion of his choice. Sri Krishna has declared, 'Wherever an extraordinary spiritual power is manifest, know that I am there'. So the Hindu recognizes the same God in all is prepared for many more in the future. Hinduism stands for a grand symphony of religious ideals. What it disapproves is hatred, bigotry and religious fanaticism. 'As many faiths, so many paths,' says Sri Ramakrishna, the latest Prophet of Hinduism.

SWAMI MADHAVANANDA

The Attitude of the Ramakrishna Math and Mission toward non-Hindu Religions

Swami Madhavananda is General Secretary of the Ramakrishna Mission whose world-headquarters is at Belur Math (Howrah) West Bengal, India. The Ramakrishna Math and its sister organization, the Ramakrishna Mission, were started by Swami Vivekananda for the practice and propagation of the principles of Vedanta as lived and taught by his Master, Sri Ramakrishna Paramahamsa. Swami Vivekananda participated in the World Parliament of Religions held at the Chicago World's Fair (1893) where he made a deep impression.

Vedanta preaches the oneness of evistence and the essential unity of the human soul with the supreme Godhead, Brahman, and it accepts that all religions are so many paths to God. Sri Ramakrishna realized this teaching of Vedanta in his own life, and taught that God created a diversity of religions to suit the varying tastes and capacities of different people. If there was sincerity. everyone would ultimately realize the highest truth, through the grace of the Lord, by following his chosen path. This has determined the attitude of the Ramakrishna Math and Mission towards all faiths.

These twin organizations have never subscribed to the view that only one religion can be true, for the same truth may appear as diverse to different people according to their comprehension of it. Just as the same person may be a father, a master, a husband, a brother, a son, a friend, and an enemy and so forth, to different persons, so one and the same Brahman is looked upon as the Father in Heaven, the Divine Mother, the Lord, the Friend, The Child, the Beloved, the Supreme Soul and so on, by different people. Hence there is no contradiction in different religions presenting the same ultimate Reality in different ways. The Supreme Principle includes all these aspects, and is infinitely more.

Among the earliest rules laid down by Swami Vivekananda for the Ramakrishna Math was the following: "Due respect and reverence should be paid to all religions, all preachers, and to the deities worshipped in all religions." And the declaration which all intending members of the Ramakrishna Mission have to give begins as follows: "I look upon Sri Ramakrishna as an illustration and embodiment of the Religion Eternal, whoce life and teachings help one to understand the plan and purpose of all the religions of the world and their underlying truth and harmony. I look upon all religions as paths to God, and shall try to live in peace and fellowship with the followers of all religions."

Not merely toleration, but acceptance of all religions is the watchword of the Ramakrishna Math and Mission. In the memorial temple of Sri Ramakrishna at the Belur Math, in West Bengal, the headquarters of the organization, the followers of all religions are equally welcome, and like the Hindu religious festivals, Christmas Eve and Lord Buddha's Birthday are also devoutly observed there and in the important branch centers. The medical and educational institutions of the Order, its classes and lectures, as also its relief works are open to all, irrespective of religion, since the Order looks upon these activities as the service of God in man. Its one aim has ever been to help all in a spirit of brotherly love to regain their dimmed – but not lost – perfection, by trying in its humble way to remove the veils, physical, intellectual and spiritual, that are thwarting its manifestation.

D. M. BOSE

The Brahmo Samaj

The Brahmo Samaj, whose Secretary, Dr. Bose, has contributed this statement, was founded in 1828 by Ramohan Roy (1772–1833). Like his two great predecessors, Nanak and Kabir, he was led by his many-sided endowments and his religious sensibilities, coupled with his deep human sympathies, to study the sacred writings of ancient India and of Islam. The monotheism he preached contained elements derived from both, as well as from his study of the Christian scriptures. To this monotheism he added a knowledge of 18th century European humanitarianism and enlightenment and thus became the pioneer of the modern age in India.

The Brahmo Samaj is a Society of the worshippers of the One God of all religions and all humanity. It recognizes the importance of a congregational form of worship. Its founders, growing out of the religious heritage of India, exercised their religious intuition and critical judgment in accepting what they considered to be the Hindu monotheism, into which they incorporated the theistic elements of the two other great world religions – a synthesis possible only in the tolerant religious tradition of India.

The Brahmo Samaj believes that the core of religious truth – the unity of God as spirit, his worship in spirit and in truth, the immortality of the soul, and ethical discipline as the basis of spiritual life – form the central teaching of the historic religions. There is only one Theism with certain historical varieties, e.g. a Hindu theism, an Islamic theism, and a Christian theism.

The Brahmo Samaj includes Hindu, Moslem and Christian theism in one theistic fraternity as brothers in faith; it extends its fellowship and cooperation to those who, by whatever name, acknowledge some Principle of the Universe, the need of meditation on that Principle as good, and the love and service of man as the Principle of the conduct of life. Buddhists and Jains and believers in a Law of Nature are acknowledged as not against the theistic fraternity but with it.

The Brahmo Samaj accepts, respects and uses the scriptures of the world, not as infallible supernatural revelations, but as ancient records of the moral and spiritual life and progress of man; and it honours all true prophets and teachers of humanity, not as specific incarnations or mediators, but as manifestations, within the necessary limitations of their own time and race, of the nature of God, in whose image and out of whose substance humanity is created.

The Brahmo Samaj accepts that the Universal Truth was stressed in different ways, had different accents in different historical utterances. For a synthesis, each religion, while preserving its own historical or traditional continuity, should free itself from all accretions of beliefs, customs and rituals, which in the light of progressive development of the spiritual and ethical insight of man, has been judged to be erroneous and degrading, and should grow by mutual contact and assimilation, and by convergence to a common ideal.

CHANDRASEKHARENDRA SARASVATI SWAMI

Fundamental Unity of Hinduism

His Holiness Sri Jagadguru Sri Chandrasekharendra Sarasvati is Sankaracharya of Kanchi Kamakoti Pitam. As an authoritative spokesman of a Hindu sect, he calls for unity. This is an excerpt from "The Call of the Jagadguru", published by Ganesh & Co. in Madras.

Unity in variety is the secret of life and religion. Every vision of truth that man has is a vision of God and of none else. This is the only recognition of universality that is possible and reasonable. In the name of Universality that is possible and reasonable. In the name of Universal Religion, let us not abolish all existing religions. Rather let us try to deepen and intensify every man's fath in his own Ishta Devata or chosen deity. Let his love for his own particular God deepen and he will cease to look down with contempt on his neighbor's religious ideals. And when sects and religions have thus broadened, their power for good will have increased hundredfold. What is really needed is a fellow-feeling between the different sects, a fellow-feeling which springs from mutual esteem, understanding and a rediscovery of their common bases.

Let us promote unity in our ranks, deepen the faith in our religion, realize the basic harmony that runs through the different sects within the bosom of Hinduism and catch the mystic whisper of the heavenly music of our religious classics. Then it will be possible for us to give to the world the message of universal religion. Has our religion today the hidden strength for such a noble destiny? It is for us to build up our spiritual strength and generate a new idealism, a true child of the nation's past, with which the young should throb and the old should be reverent.

CHANDRASEKHARA BHARATI SWAMI

Universality of Religion

His Holiness Sri Chandrasekhara Bharati Swami, Late Sankaracharya of Sringeri Mutt, was another advocate of greater unity and universality in religion. The following "Conversation between His Holiness and a European Gentleman" is taken from "Dialogues with the Guru" by R. Krishnaswami Aiyar, published by Chetana, Ltd., Bombay.

E.G.   Swamiji, may I know if you are prepared to take in converts to your religion? Personally, I find much worth in it and I have known very many friends who so love your philosophy and religion that they would like to call themselves Hindus, if that were possible.

H.H.   The Hindu system of philosophy and religion is bound to attract all thinking mends, but we do not take in converts.

E.G.   If you think that your system is an invaluable one and is bound to be useful to all mankind, does it not follow that you must be prepared to take in converts?

H.H.   Not necessarily. Conversion is possible or necessary only when the person who desires to be a convert does not already belong to the religion to which he desires to be converted.

E.G.   How is that? Do you mean to say that no formal conversion is necessary as those who desire to be Hindus are already Hindus by virtue of that desire itself?

H.H.   No. I mean that all are Hindus irrespective of their desire to be called Hindus.

E.G.   How can that be?

H.H.   Hinduism is the name which has now been given to our system, but its real name has always been Sanatana Dharma or the Eternal Law. It does not date from a particular point of time or begin from a particular founder. Being eternal, it is also universal. It knows no territorial jurisdiction. All beings born and to be born belong to it. They cannot escape this law, whether they concede its binding force or not. The eternal law that fire burns does not depend for its validity upon our allegiance to it. If we accept that truth, so much the better for us. If we do not, so much the worse for us. In either case, the law is there, immutable, universal and eternal. Such is our Sanatana Dharma.

E.G.   I have tried to understand Christianity and follow it to the best of my lights but very many doubts are cropping up now and then and I have not been able to meet anybody who can solve them. That is why I wanted to study other religions.

H.H. Doubts can never be solved unless you approach the persons who have not merely studied their religion but are daily living it. For the purpose of trade, you are prepared to cross the seas and explore the air, but for the purpose of Truth you want the teachers to come to your door and solve your doubts for you. The attitude that religion is an interesting side aspect of life must go. If once you realize that religion is life itself and not an aspect of it, you will begin to explore the entire world earnestly for a proper teacher. He is ever available and is but waiting for a symptom of real earnestness in you. I am not prepared to believe that there are no such teachers in Christianity. They may not be in the ordinary world of strife, for such a world does not want them nor have they any use for such a world. They may sometimes be found even in the midst of strife, as strife cannot injure them. Go, therefore, in search of such true Christians and ask them in true humbleness of heart to solve your doubts. They will do so in no time and you will find that God, in spite of your doubts, was after all justified in making you the child of Christian parents.

E.G. I cannot sufficiently thank you, Swamiji, for your kind words of advice. Please allow me to confess that when I came here I had no idea that I would be going away from you with a sincere desire to be a better Christian. But that is the desire which you have inculcated in me. If your aim is to make a Christian a better Christian, a Hindu a better Hindu, and so on, your religion is certainly more catholic than I thought it was. In parting, may I have your gracious blessing?

SUBRAHMANIA DESIKA
GNANASAMBANDHA PARAMACARYA
SWAMIGAL

The Lord Siva in Worldly Life

His Holiness, the author of the following message, is the Head of the *Dharmapuram Math*, a well-known center of devotion to Siva, in the Tanjore District of South India. His identification of religion with the life of service is intended to apply not only to the particular devotion to the Lord Siva, which he represents, but to religion generally.

Religion enables our worldly life to develop along fruitful lines. Religion is blended in the lives of all of us. In every act, from the act of lighting a lamp to offering worship, the impress of religion is to be found. Those who nurtured religion are called the religious forbears. Our religious forbears are Tirugnanasambandhar, Tirunavukkarasar, Sundaramurti Swamigal and Manikkavacaga Swamigal. The religious forbears devoted themselves to service, not only in the religious sphere but also in the secular one. The biographies of Sambandhar and Appar (Tirunavukkarasar) reveal their service in the secular field. With the noble aim of wishing to share with mankind their spiritual joy, they gave us the devotional works. We can never forget that time and again they came to the rescue of people in distress, relieved their suffering and brought them happiness – all out of their great compassion. Alike in weal and woe, religion stood as a source of great help. The inner meaning of deed, classified as 'para' (higher) and 'apara' (lower) would show that religion and wordly life are not different....

The temples where the Lord resides as melody, fruition, and as Nadabrahman, (Sound-Brahman) are not only places for the nurture of religion: they have also served as schools, hospitals, art centres for the development of sculpture, painting, music, dance and drama, and as courts of justice. People who lost their homes in cyclones and floods have survived death by taking refuge in the temple. In many similar ways, religion has blended with the lives of the people.

Long live Grace! May religion prosper!

SHRIMAD ANANDASHRAM SWAMIJI

Hinduism and Eternal Religion

His Holiness Sri Anandashram Swamiji of Sri Chitrapur Math in Southern India is the religious head of the Sarasvats, a well-known branch of popular Hinduism.

The characteristically Hindu attitude toward other religions derives from a few simple human considerations of general validity. First comes the realization that the experience of unity is as indisputable a fact as that of multiplicity or diversity. From this it naturally follows that any concept of reality should comprehend both, and provide for their co-existence. One-sidedness is to be avoided at all costs. The pairs of opposites *(dvandvas)* form the warp and woof of normal human experience. It is by transcending them that they can be resolved, not by partisanship.

The next point is the appreciation of the inadequacy and relativity of all verbal expression. Real communication by means of words becomes possible only when the mental backgrounds of the speaker and the listener are *en rapport* with each other, as for example, in the combination of the ideal teacher *(Guru)* and disciple. Propositional statements divorced from their human context cannot but be a prolific source of misunderstanding and controversy. Reality lends itself to being variously described: as the Rigveda puts it, "Reality is one: Sages call it by various names." In its essence, Reality is such that words recoil from it and mind cannot compass it. It can be reached only in the intimacy of existential bliss *(Ananda)* which is identical with freedom from all fears. "He who knows the bliss of Brahman, whence words together with the mind turn away, unable to reach it – he is not afraid of anything whatsoever."

These considerations, inbred in the Hindu temperament, rather than consciously held, have coloured the Hindu outlook through and through. "Live and let live" has been the cherished motto. A respectful tolerance has been its dominating feature; not the patronizing condescension of those who claim to be in exclusive possession of the truth. Through the centuries, there has been a marked absence of propaganda or of any desire to convert others. That one may reach God through the practice of one's own religion is the very essence of Hinduism.

The apparent multiplicity of the Vedic gods was superimposed on an identity of background and a certain interchangeability of attributes which puzzled foreigners; and scholars had to coin a new term to express this: henotheism, which they attempted to define as the doctrine that there is among gods a supreme God for any particular religious faith. Within the fold of Hinduism, the utmost freedom of worship is its most notable characteristic. Sri Krishna says in the Gita that by whatever path devotees approach Him, He meets them half-way. This is the doctrine of *Ishtadevatā* (Chosen Ideal) which takes into account the inbred differences among individuals and provides for congenial modes of approach, depending on fitness *(Adhikāra)*. Hence the prevalence of all levels of practice and understanding, and of all possible permutations and combinations of religious experience.

This freedom is universally valid, for the Hindu as well as for the non-Hindu. That is really why there is no such thing as "Hinduism" but only the *Sanātana Dharma*, Eternal Religion.

CHAPTER FIVE

ISLAM

Norms on Inter-religious relations Given in the Koran

(Selected with an introduction by Professor Syed Vahiduddin
of Osmania University, Hyderabad, India)

Islam's attitude toward life is founded on the basic concepts of the
Koran, and these concepts are not speculative abstractions without any
relation to the historical existence of man, but live even today with all
the dynamic vitality in the consciousness of the believers, and mold their
pattern of day-to-day life. It is first of all the vision of God who encom-
passes and surpasses all existence, and who is the creator and sustainer
of not only the tiny world known to us, but of worlds without number.
Though unknowable in His transcendental essence, He is named with
different names in His revelation to man. Above all, He is all compassion
and mercy. Every *surah* of the Koran begins with an emphasis on this
ever-present attribute.

The Koran allows no compulsion in religion, and enjoins its followers
not to be led to injustice by the hatred and ill-will their enemies might
provoke in them. Aggression is condemned in no mistakable terms, and
when fighting is allowed it is allowed with great reluctance and as a last
measure. What is called *jihad* is really a struggle, a struggle against the
evil that prevails around and about, and more than that a struggle against
the evil that lurks in all of us, as it is indicated in a tradition attributed to
the prophet. The people who carry the message of their religion may
deviate from its teaching in their historical progress, but the religion, as
such, is unequivocal in what it inculcates.

The verses given below bear an eloquent testimony to the claim of
Islam as a religion of surrender to God without any reservation and as
the peace that is born of it. Indeed, as a religion it is seriously concerned
to lift man from the injustice which he often inflicts on himself and from
the bestiality into which he is prone to fall to the true humanity in which
he is the vice-regent of Allah on earth and attuned with His will.

II–*62* "Lo! those who believe (in that which is revealed unto thee,
Muhammad), and those who are Jews, and Christians, and Sabaeans

– whoever believeth in Allah and the Last Day and doeth right – surely their reward is with their Lord, and there shall no fear come upon them neither shall they grieve."

II–*112* "Nay, but whosoever surrendereth his purpose to Allah while doing good, his reward is with his Lord; and there shall no fear come upon them neither shall they grieve."

II–*177* "It is not righteousness that ye turn your faces to the East and the West; but righteous is he who believeth in Allah and the Last Day and the angels and the Scripture and the Prophets; and giveth his wealth for love of Him, to kinsfolk and to orphans and the needy and the wayfarer and to those who ask, and to set slaves free; and observeth proper worship and payeth the poor-due. And those who keep their treaty when they make one, and the patient in tribulation and adversity and time of stress. Such are they who are sincere. Such are the God-fearing."

V–*8* O ye who believe! Be steadfast witnesses for Allah in equity, and let not hatred of any people seduce you that ye deal not justly. Deal justly, that is nearer to your duty. Observe your duty to Allah. Lo! Allah is informed of what you do."

XI–*85* "O my people! Give full measure and full weight in justice, and wrong not people in respect of their goods. And do not evil in the earth, causing corruption.

II–*190* "Fight in the way of Allah against those who fight against you, but begin not hostilities. Lo! Allah loveth not aggressors."

III–*133* "And vie one with another for forgiveness from your Lord, and for a Paradise as wide as are the heavens and the earth, prepared for those who ward off (evil); *134* Those who spend (of that which Allah hath given them) in ease and in adversity, those who control their wrath and are forgiving toward mankind; Allah loveth the good; *135* And those who, when they do an evil thing or wrong themselves, remember Allah and implore forgiveness for their sins – Who forgiveth sins save Allah only? – and will not knowingly repeat (the wrong) they did."

IV–*1* "O mankind! Be careful of your duty to your Lord Who created you from a single soul and from it created its mate and from them twain hath spread abroad a multitude of men and women. Be careful of your duty toward Allah in Whom ye claim (your rights) of one another, and toward the wombs (that bare you) Lo! Allah hath been a Watcher over you."

IV–*94* "O ye who believe! When ye go forth (to fight) in the way of Allah, be careful to discriminate, and say not unto one who offereth you peace: "Thou art not a believer," seeking the chance profits of this life (so that ye may despoil him). With Allah are plenteous spoils. Even thus (as he now is) were ye before; but Allah hath since then been gracious unto you. Therefore take care to discriminate. Allah is ever Informed of what ye do."

XI–*85* "O my people! Give full measure and full weight in justice, and wrong not people in respect of their goods. And do not evil in the earth, causing corruption."

XVI–*90* Lo! Allah enjoineth justice and kindness, and giving to kins-folk, and forbiddeth lewdness and abomination and wickedness. He exhorteth you in order that ye may take heed."

From *The Meaning of the Glorious Koran*

MUHAMMAD HAMIDULLAH

Islam and the Non-Muslim World

The Author of this statement for the Handbook is a professor at the University of Paris. He is widely recognized as a scholarly interpreter of Muslim Traditions (Hadith) and as a modern expounder of Muslim doctrine. He reflects especially the Islam of South-east Asia.

It goes without saying that if a religion were to admit any of its prede-cessors as entirely sufficient for the eternal salvation of mankind, it would be in a self-contradictory position, for the very *raison d'etre* of this new religion would be underminded. However, the Quran repeats again and again, that it is not intended to create a new religion, but only to confirm and revive the former religions which were based on divine revelations. While naming over a score of these, the Quran affirms that everywhere messengers of God have appeared to guide particular groups. The essence of the divine message remains always the same; it may vary in details, due to the varied development of human mentality. That message is the submission of man to the will of the One God; this is the meaning of the word "Islam". As the divinely revealed books have been suffering at the hands of man, mostly on account of pagan invasions, which have caused the destruction of documents containing the divine revelations, God, in His mercy, has been sending again and again new messengers. Muham-mad taught what Adam, Abraham, Moses or Jesus had taught. Since the Quran has been preserved to posterity in its entirety and original form, there is no need for a new messenger.

In his famous letter, addressed to Heraclius and some other Christian princes of his time, Muhammad cited a verse of the Quran (3:64): "O people of the Scripture, come to a single word, the same for us and you; that we shall worship none but God, and that we shall ascribe no partners unto Him, and that none of us shall take others for lords beside God." In another well-known verse, the Quran affirms twice (2:62; 5:69): "Lo! Those who believe, and those who are Jews, and Christians, and Sabaeans – Whoever believeth in God and the Last Day, and doeth right – surely their reward is with their Lord, and there shall no fear come upon them neither shall they grieve." On the basis of these elements, which seem to lay down the minimum necessary for salvation, for a basic religion, Mr. Marmaduke Pickthall, who was a very pious and orthodox Muslim, had concluded that if Jews, Christians, etc. practice charity in a God-fearing manner, they will receive salvation. Other Muslim scholars and divines however, would not go so far, and they refer to yet another verse of the Quran (4:150) which says that to believe only in God and not in His messenger is no belief.

Islam distinguishes between those non-Muslims who nevertheless possess a divinely revealed Book, and those who do not. A Muslim is authorized to eat an animal slaughtered by the former but not otherwise. Further, a Muslim may marry a girl of the first category, and not of the other. Of course, untouchability or segregation, on account of religion or race, are unknown to Islam. The Quranic injunction that polytheists should no more approach the Kaabah was interpreted by Caliph Umar to mean that they should not be allowed to use the Kaabah as their temple for idolatry; and he once received a Christian plaintiff while delivering a Friday sermon in the mosque of the Kaabah, as has been reported by Abu Yusuf.

It is well-known that the Quran enjoins complete judicial and juridical autonomy for non-Muslim residents of a Muslim territory, a practice which was in full force down to the First World War, and which still continues with slight variations in most Muslim countries.

It is the Quran which enjoins on Muslims to give quarter and asylum to any non-Muslim who asks it and not to extradite him except for his safety. It is also the Quran which enjoins its adherents scrupulously to observe treaties concluded with non-Muslims. As to cooperation for charitable purposes, suffice it to quote the verse (5:2) of the Quran: "... and let not your hatred of a folk who stopped you going to the Sacred Mosque (of the Kaabah) seduce you to transgress; but help ye one another unto righteousness and pious duty; help not one another unto sin and transgression but keep your duty to God; lo, God is severe in punishment." When this is prescribed for those who are actually at war, it is easy to imagine what should be the Muslim attitude toward those who are at peace.

It is well-known that the Quran formally forbids compelling anybody to embrace Islam. Like some of their predecessors, Muslims too have laid down the law that a Muslim may not renounce his religion without the threat of sanctions. This is worth explaining, even though the actual cases are extremely rare, not only in Muslim states (which may fail to use the prescribed sanctions) but even in non-Muslim dominions, where systematic and very thorough attempts have been made, for centuries together, to wean them from Islam, yet in vain. Punishment of the a-postate in Islam seems to be due not on accont of religion or belief, but politics. The political conception of "nationality" in Islam is not based on the ineluctable accidents of nature, such as birthplace, mother-tongue, colour of skin; but on individual choice and deliberate will to embrace a particular pattern of life. In this perspective, apostasy is simply political infidelity, which is, as elsewhere, considered to be treason. That is the law. As the cases are extremely rare, the question of practical application has not raised complications.

I must say, there is a false and perhaps malicious interpretation of the Islamic "*Jihad*" in some circles. Its right translation is not "holy war", but struggle. To compel others to embrace Islam is forbidden by the Quran. To struggle for the peaceful preaching of Islam is the duty of every Muslim, according to his individual capacities. No doubt a war in Islam is holy, but this does not at all mean a war waged to force others to embrace Islam. As Ghazali has so nicely explained: if one prays to God and worships Him for ostentation, it is not devotion but polytheism, worship of the self; on the other hand, if one eats to have strength enough to carry out duties laid down by God, if one has intercourse with his wife with the notion that it is the performance of a divinely ordered obligation, these physical and sexual pleasures are holy, are acts of devotion and worship of God, are *ibadah*. In the same way, a justi-fiable war is holy, but a war waged to compel others to embrace Islam is never so.

Unlike some other religious communities of the contemporary world, the reform movements among Muslims are mostly a call for "back to the original purity." The latest authoritative examples are Syria (before its merger with Egypt) and Pakistan (before its military dictatorship) whose state constitutions formally laid down the decision to revise the actual legislation, remnant of the days of colonial yoke, in order to make it conform with the teachings of the Quran and the Hadith.

The *jizyah*, a scutage tax, was common in the Middle Ages, yet for many centuries it has not been imposed. When the recent Constitution of Pakistan was in preparation, its *Majlis Ta-limat Islamiyah*, (a very pious council, *ulema*, attached to the Constituent Assembly) suggested that the *jizyah* did not seem to be an integral part of Islam. They argued that the Prophet himself was disposed to exempt certain non-Muslims from this tax; that the Caliph Umar had in fact exempted from time to time, some non-Muslim subjects from paying this tax, on account of their meritorious services rendered to the State; they also referred to possible repercussions on Muslim subjects of non-Muslim states today, Jewish, Christian, Hindu and others.

It is intersting to note that many a Muslim State exchanged an Ambassador with the Vatican and that the Patriarch of the Orthodox Church was allowed to remain in Istanbul even after the rebellion of Greece against the Ottoman Empire and its secession from it. He continues to reside there even today.

When there was a mass exodus of the Hindus and the Sikhs from Pakistan in 1957 (parallel to similar movements of Muslims from India), no temples or shrines were touched, which remain even today, in the absence of their devotees, under government protection.

The Muslim state of Hyderabad had, while independent, several features of interest to our theme. It had organized a *Majlis Muqtadayan-i-Madhahib* (Council of the Chiefs of Religions), in which high personalities of Muslim, Hindu, Sikh, Parsi, Christian and other religions participated on terms of equality, which won the esteem of the public as well as of the government. It used to send every year, at government expense, not only a certain number of poor Muslims on pilgrimage to Mecca, but also a similar number of Hindus to visit their own shrines and places of pilgrimage. In its University, not only the birthday of Muhammad, but also of Sri Krishna, was solemnly celebrated every year by all the students, irrespective of their religions. In this connection prize essays were written every year on given topics. Special prizes were reserved for non-Muslim students, competing in the essay on the life of Muhammad, and vice versa. The government had instituted special scholarships for Hindus studying Arabic as their optional subject, and Muslims the Sanscrit language, etc.

In Paris, there is a *Centre Culturel Islamique*, composed of Muslims living in Paris. Among its several activities, it celebrates every year the

birth of Jesus Christ, as the anniversary of one of the great messengers
of God common to Islam and Christianity. On this occasion, it sends gift
parcels of provisions to poor Christians on behalf of the Muslim community.[1]

M. HAFIZ SYED

Islam and Other Faiths

The author is professor at the Muslim University of Allahabad, India,
and is known as an authority on the Sufi movement in Islam. However,
his statement refers to Islam generally and not to any sectarian group.

In each religion one must distinguish between the principles laid down
by the founders and the manner in which their followers live up to them.
Hence, to judge a religion by the comparative indifference of a majority
of its followers would not be fair to the principles. The present-day religion of Islam, as known and practiced by its followers, has been greatly
misunderstood and misinterpreted. Islam and its Founder have always
preached good will and toleration towards the members of other faiths.
They have distinctly enjoined in the Holy Quran, that there is to be no
compulsion in religion, and that every one should be free to follow his
way of life provided he lives and lets others live unhindered and un-
interfered with. But the history of the Muslims in different parts of the
world tells a different tale. Some of them have been guilty of fanaticism,
intolerance and persecution. For all this, Islam itself should not be blamed.

It must be conceded that the Prophet of Islam did, now and then, engage
in warfare with his neighbouring communities. But he never waged an
offensive war. All through his brilliant career he was compelled by the
prevailing circumstances to defend himself and his followers. Unlike
those of other teachers, the details of his life are scrupulously preserved.
His attitude toward the Jews and the Christians was always friendly and
brotherly. He treated them with utmost kindness and consideration, as
is chronicled by non-Muslim writers and historians.

Our prophet not only proclaimed the fact of universal human brotherhood, but for the first time in the history of the world, made it a principle
and fact of common law. All the ordinances of Islam tend toward it, and
it is shown to be the only ground of genuine human progress. Social

---

[1] Among the publications of this institution, there is an *Introduction to Islam*, in
the English language, containing a chapter on the "Status of non-Muslims in Islam".
This book may also be obtained from the Mosque in Washington, D.C.

inequality remained; retained were those restrictions upon individual liberty which must exist in every organized society. But brotherly relations were established permanently between men and nations, however different in character, rank, wealth or power. "The slaves who say their prayers are your brothers". And it was no mere pious phrase. They were actually so treated. In the intercourse between nations, also, there was established a brotherhood which still endures. The spirit of aggressive nationality was abolished among Muslims by our Prophet's saying:

"He is not of us who sides with his tribe in aggression, and he is not one of us who calls others to help him in tyranny, and he is not one of us who dies while assisting his tribe in injustice."

Islam became a super-nationality which extinguished nationalism in the body of Islam and characterized as madness the idea of a man's fighting for "his country right or wrong". Our Prophet said that an Ethiopian slave who does right is more worthy to be made the ruler than a Sharif of Quraish who does wrong. Social service was acknowledged as the strongest claim to the respect and reverence of the community, a claim much stronger than the claim of birth or riches or brute force. Race and colour prejudices disappeared completely in the Muslim brotherhood, and differences of class were purged of either arrogance or humiliation, and reduced to mere differences of occupation. Islamic civilization is a complete system, covering every field of human thought and action, from the spiritual to the menial- a system which has been found successful in practice. It is a brotherhood composed not of a single class or nation but of many classes and many nations.

The Islamic brotherhood should be the model of a true League of Nations, for here the people are at heart united. Scattered though the Muslim realm has been politically, the solidarity of the peoples remains unimpaired, unbroken.

Some critics, seeing it hold firm against all pressure from without, exclaim: "The Muslims even when they pretend to be nationalists have no patriotism, only fanaticism."

Islam's attitude towards other faiths is determined by explicit Quranic teachings. The fundamental right of all faiths to exist in complete freedom is established unequivocally by the injunction: "There shall be no compulsion in the matter of religion." "Verily those who believe, and those who keep the Jews' religious rule and the Christians' and the Sabaeans – whosoever believeth in Allah and the Last Day, and doeth right – their reward is with their Lord; and there shall no fear come upon them, neither shall they suffer grief." (The Quran)

It is a misreading of the defensive fight of the Prophet to think that he wanted to compel even the idolatrous pagan tribes of Arabia to accept his faith at the point of the sword. For more than a decade the Muslims tried a policy of leaving these tribes alone if they but would let the Muslims follow their new faith in peace, on the principle of live and let live. It was only after this policy had failed that the Prophet, in the words of Carlyle, was compelled to stand up like a man and like an Arab to defend the liberty of his faith by using necessary force against force. Against the brutal savage tribes the principles of peaceful persuasion and toleration could not work. Islam would have been destroyed, if these barbarous hordes had not been curbed by force. Their mentality was such that they invaded Medina, the nucleus of the incipient Muslim State, immediately after the death of the Prophet, even though they had submitted to the political power of Islam, ostensibly, during the life of the Prophet. It was the faith and courage of a few heroes that met successfully this counter-revolutionary onslaught. The Prophet was peace-loving and tolerant to the last towards those who left him and his followers in peace. He returned to Mecca, from whence he and his followers had been driven after persistent persecution, and merely a show of force subdued his enemies.

The Prophet made great efforts to convince the Jews and Christians that he was carrying forward only the eternal message of Abraham, Moses, and Jesus, large-heartedly showering praises on them and appreciating their scriptures as divinely revealed and as sources of Light and Life, accepting them as Messengers of One God. He wanted these theistic communities to live in peace with the Muslims on the basis of that which is, or ought to be, a common ground of agreement for all of them. This common ground of agreement, proposed by the Prophet, includes nothing more than the belief in One God, common to all theists, and in the equality of man before God, no man accepting other men or classes as Lords over him. Even though the proposal was not accepted, the Muslims were enjoined to create as many bonds of love and good will between themselves and the theistic communities as possible. It was impossible to create any bonds of love with the polytheistic pagan tribes, so they were left out for the time being; but with respect to the Jews and Christians, who had so much in common with the Muslims, the Quran advised the Muslims to have intimate social relations with them, to eat and drink with them; and it was made lawful to marry Jewish and Christian women without compelling them to adopt the Muslim faith. Good Christians have been particularly praised in the Quran as nearest to the Muslims in faith and sympathy.

Justice is prescribed equally for all, Muslim or non-Muslim, friend or foe. No dual standards either in morals or in law are allowed or tolerated. No aggression is permitted. There are many verses in the Quran repeating with emphasis that God does not love aggressors. The basic ideology of Islam is not only liberty for all faiths but their protection in the socio-political sphere. What Islam stands for is evident in the following verse:

"If God had not raised a group to ward off aggression, churches, synagogues, temples and mosques, where God is worshipped most, would have been destroyed."

It is noteworthy that in a scripture that is promulgating Islam, the defence of the places of worship of others is mentioned before the mosques. The defence of one's own place of worship is natural and is rooted in the psychology of groups; being self-evident, the concern for the mosque is expressed after the places of worship of the other creeds, which requires a total reorientation of the religious mind. It was on account of this concern for other creeds and their liberties that during the early battles of Islam, when armies were ordered to march against the enemies, they were instructed not to touch any non-combatant or old men, women and children and to take special care that no priest of another creed was injured nor any place of worship desecrated.

The Prophet did not debar Christians from praying in his own mosque. Once a Christian deputation, while conversing with him in his mosque, said their time for prayer had arrived and proposed that they should leave; but the Prophet asked them to stay on and say their prayer in his mosque.

The Quran has said that humanity shall never follow one single creed, and therefore, rituals and dogmas and modes of worship shall continue to differ; but notwithstanding this variety, every creed in its own way should strive towards the maximum realization of the good; they should compete with each other only in this common effort.

CHAPTER SIX

JUDAISM

LEO JUNG

The Attitude of Judaism toward Other Religions

Rabbi Jung of New York City is recognized as a leading spokesman for Orthodox Judaism in the United States.

Fundamentally, as far as the attitude of one religion to another is concerned, the choice lies between ethical universalism and church universalism. According to the former, every member of religions which emphasize the obligations of ethical living, though their conceptions of God may differ, is capable of eternal salvation. According to the latter, salvation is reserved for the members of a universal church. Once such church universalism is laid down, subdivision of the human family comes automatically and further divisiveness follows as the night the day.

Judaism eithteen hundred years ago, made a definite statement: No matter what the individual's dogma or creed, so long as God is the centre of his belief and the standard for his practice, he enjoys in Israel equality of worth, brotherhood of civic rights and eternal acceptance, whatever be his philosophy of ultimate reality. Judaism has thus agreed to disagree in matters theological, recognizing the value and dignity of the individual outside the synagogue and extending to him, in the name of God and His sanctuary, the natural right to serve his Master in accord with his own conscience.

According to Dr. Isidore Epstein, one of the foremost authorities of orthodox Judaism, "Provided there is no idolatry, which Judaism condemns not so much because it is a false religion as because it is a false morality, humanity as a whole is not charged to accept the conception of Hebrew monotheism."

In order that organized religion achieve its social purpose, it is essential not only to emphasize in the clearest and broadest form the universal principles which guide it, but to distinguish also between the forces of irreligion and the causes which have made this generation veer from the ancient moorings. The momentum of modern dissent is to a considerable extent due to the failure of organized religion to present a factual demonstration of, or even a general disposition toward, true love, forebearance, tolerance for peace, and passion for the under-dog. Too often has it seemed to spell but conventional respectability. It has gone hand in hand with reaction; it has been found inarticulate in the presence of the normal phenomenon of mass misery side by side with heartbreaking luxury. Recognition of human equality, independent of geographical or any other differences, is of paramount need not only among the citizens of a state or country, but especially among adherents of the various religions. Not only will such practical acknowledgement in no measure reduce the importance of any denomination to its members, but, by conveying the sense of the core of all religion – brotherhood of man under the Fatherhood of God – it will immeasurably strengthen loyalty to one's own creed and thus the forces for good and the influence of religion. Surely, in the minds of thoughtful members, the individual religions could surrender part of their organizational sovereignty in order to advance the acceptance, in theory and practice, of the sovereignty of religion for all men.

The texts by which the religious life of the pious Jew is guided, have made this principle very clear: "Every pious person in the world has, in truth, imbibed the milk of mother Sarah" and "Whosoever rejects the practices of idolatry resembles him who observes the whole Torah." Hence every human being shall be treated humanely, fed if hungry, cured if sick, and provided with a grave when found dead and unattended. Throughout Rabbinic literature, even during times of cruel persecution, the importance of these duties was never forgotten. The thirteenth century moralist Jacob Anatoli stated: "We are not so foolish and arrogant as to claim that we alone possess a portion of God's spirit. We shall not fall into the error of those who insist that they alone breathe the breath divine, and that a Jew has no soul. We believe that the image of God is indelibly stamped upon all men." The seventeenth century great Rabbi Jonathan Eibeschutz considers the promotion of good will between Jews and non-Jews a major individual and communal obligation. These principles have retained their authority to the present day. They should be considered an ever-ready potent source for constructive cooperation between Judaism and other religions in many areas, social and cultural, in which joint effort is urgently needed.

ABBA HILLEL SILVER
The Relation of Judaism to Other Religions

Rabbi Silver of Cleveland, Ohio is recognized as an influential spokesman for Reform Judiasm and as a leader of Jewish community life.

Judaism is a universalistic faith in the stewardship of a people which
regarded itself as bound to this faith by an historic covenant. The people
of Israel was committed to carry its universal God idea and all that flows
from it in terms of human brotherhood, justice, and peace, to the whole
of mankind. It accepted a specific discipline and a way of life, defined
in the Torah, in order to insure the effective accomplishment of this
mission. This discipline did not interfere with its universal spiritual and
ethical doctrines which were never monopolized by the Jewish people.
They were offered freely to the whole world. All men, regardless of race
or status were welcomed into the faith. Some of Israel's foremost leaders
and teachers were descendants of proselytes, including King David, to
whom later ages traced the lineage of the Messiah.

Non-Jews who were not prepared to accept the full discipline, inclusive
of customs and ceremonial laws, were nevertheless welcomed as "God-
fearers." Their status was regarded as in no way inferior to that of the
full-fledged members of the household of Israel. Judaism never claimed
to be the one and only channel for salvation. Rather, it held to the conviction that "the righteous among the gentiles will have a portion in the
world to come." (Tosefta, Sanhedrin 13.2)

Its dominant hope was not to convert the whole world to Judaism but
to convert the whole world to God. The one universal God does not
require one universal church in which to be worshipped, but a universal
devotion. Accordingly, though Judaism was determined to preserve its
own spiritual identity, undiminished, in a world which was given over to
powerful syncretistic tendencies, it never isolated itself spiritually, except
in periods of persecution when isolation was in fact forced upon it, or
when the surrounding cultures were found to be morally noxious and a
menace to its own essential values.

While Judaism remained constantly aware of its own unique and revolutionary character, it never rejected opportunities to cooperate with
other faiths in the building of the good society, firm in its own convictions,
reverent of theirs, nor did it question their positive role in the divine plan
of history. Maimonides and other leaders regarded Jesus, as well as
Mohammed, as divine instruments in preparing the way for the universal
conversion of mankind to faith in the one true God. Judaism developed

through the ages its own characteristic style, as it were, its own view of
life, its code and forms of worship. It possesses its own traditions based
on Torah and covenant. Its adherents today find inspiration and spiritual
contentment in it, as did their fathers before them, and they wish to continue its historic identity within the configuration of other religious
cultures.

Other religions, too, have developed their charcteristic ways based on
their unique traditions and experiences. There is much which all religions
have in common and much which differentiates them. Their common
purpose in the world will not be advanced by merger or amalgamation.
Were all arts, philosphies, and religions cast into one mold, mankind
would be the poorer for it. Unwillingness to recognize differences in
religions is no evidence of broadmindedness. To ignore these differences
is to overlook the deep cleavages which existed in the past and to assume
a similarity of doctrine and outlook which does not exist in the present.
The attempt to gloss over these differences as a gesture of goodwill is a
superficial act which serves neither the purposes of scholarship nor the
realities of the situation. It is far better and more practical to look for
ways of working together on the basis of a forthright recognition of dis-
similarities rather than on a fictitious assumption of identity.

Loyalty to one's own faith can be, and should be, part of a larger
loyalty to faith generally. There are great areas of common interests in
which all religions can cooperate in mutual helpfulness and respect, influ-
encing one another and learning from one another.

MILTON STEINBERG

Jews and Non-Jews

Rabbi Steinberg speaks as a representative of Conservative Judaism
(as distinguished from Orthodox and Reform). The following statement
is taken with minor revisions from his book, *Basic Judaism*, (New York;
Harcourt, Brace & Co., 1947, pp.-98-104).

According to Jewish tradition, all men, regardless of race, religion, or
nationality, are equally God's children, equally precious in His sight,
equally entitled to justice and mercy at the hands of their fellows.
Except by virtue of character and conduct, no man is better than
any other.

Wherefore, Judaism claims no superiorities whatsoever for Jews, at
least none that are inherent to them. It does assert that they enjoy certain

advantages, the nature of their religious heritage, for example, or what
the ancient rabbis used to call "the merits of the fathers"; that is to say,
the group patrimony of faith and goodness accumulated through the ages
and available to each new generation. But these are social, cultural advantages which have to be accepted and exploited by the individual, or
they are of no account. Neither in them nor anywhere else in the Jewish
religion is the least suggestion of sanction for theories of racial superiorities and inferiorities.

The Judaism indeed is totally unaware of race. Though the Tradition loves
to trace the House of Israel to the Patriarchs, blood descent is no factor in
its calculations. Anyone accepting the Jewish faith becomes a "child of
Abraham our father" and a "Son of Israel" of equal worth with all others·
Nor is anyone barred from conversion because of national or ethnic
origins. Judaism has high standards for the admission of proselytes, but
they are entirely theological, ethical, ritualistic and educational. Anyone
may become a Jew; but no one has to do so in order to be saved, whether
in this world or the next.

The tradition rules explicitly: "The righteous of all peoples have their
share in the world to come." The universalism of Paul, after his conversion
to the Christian religion has been frequently commented on. According
to the Epistles of Paul: "There is neither Jew nor Greek, there is neither
bond nor free, there is neither male nor female: for ye are all one in
Christ Jesus. And if ye be Christ's, then are ye Abraham's seed, and heirs
according to the promise." But what is often overlooked in Paul's preach-
ments is the explicit condition he imposes, namely, "If ye be Christ's."
Paul's universalism applies to professed Christians only, or to put the
thesis in Paul's own unmistakable words: "He that disbelieveth shall be
condemned." Rejecting such exclusiveness, Judaism holds that any righteous person may expect whatever rewards accrue to righteousness in this
world or the next.

Indeed, from the strictly traditionalist viewpoint, there is a sense in
which Gentiles come by salvation more easily than Jews (though not so
certainly). For of a non-Jew it is required only that he conform to the
"seven commandments ordained upon the sons of Noah" which are the
principles of piety and morality conceived by the ancient rabbis as binding
on all mankind: to refrain from (1) idolatry; (2) incest and adultery; (3)
bloodshed; (4) the profanation of God's Name; (5) injustice and lawless-
ness; (6) robbery; and (7) inhumane conduct, such as cutting a limb from
a living animal. What is more, Talmudic literature is studded with in-
cidents concerning heathen who are said "to have acquired the world to

come" by single acts of extraordinary kindness and integrity. Against that, it is expected of Jews for their salvation that they shall undertake to discharge as many of the six hundred and thirteen commandments of the Torah as apply to them.

Judaism's readiness to recognize that others aside from Jews possess spiritual merit sufficient for salvation constitutes an instance of a liberalism which is not traditional in Western theology. It helps also to account for the position taken by the Jewish religion on converts, the fact that it will accept but not seek them, that indeed rabbis are instructed to dissuade would-be proselytes, receiving them only if they persist in their intention. It also implements the conviction that any good person, Jew or non-Jew, is acceptable before the Lord. Judaism lacks the postulate which serves as mainspring to the proselytizing zeal of some other communions. It does not assume that it alone can save from eternal damnation.

This unusual, almost paradoxical, attitude is in measure the product of history. Once, in the days of the Roman Empire, the Jews engaged in missionary activity energetically and on a wide scale; some of them even dreamed of converting the whole heathen world. But many of the hard-won pagans hankered after the ways they had ostensibly abandoned and were forever trying to insinuate them into Judaism. Many proved to be fair-weather believers, deserting their new faith as soon as it became an object of persecution. Many went over to other, ritually less exacting religions, notably Mithraism and Christianity. Once burned, twice careful. The present-day Jewish rule as to converts was designed to make sure of their earnestness and constancy.

The breadth of the Jewish outlook appears the more remarkable when one reflects on the frequent and savage persecutions to which Jews were subjected all through the Middle Ages. It would have been understandable, in view of their experiences, had they entertained the ambition ascribed to them by Shakespeare of executing the villany they had been taught and bettering the instruction, or had they denied all possibility of salvation to any member of the church that tormented them. That they continued to believe that any good man merits eternal bliss speaks volumes for the idealism of medieval Jews.

The Jewish modernist prefers not to put religions in contrast with one another. He is content that each has its share of verity and worth, that all have the right to be, that out of their diversity, God, man and the truth are better served in the long run. As for himself, he is at peace in Judaism. It is his own; he is bound to it as to his parents and native land. It is the faith of the people of which he is a member. It has an inexhaustible fund of special excellences. Like other faiths, it is unique and therefore irreplaceable. The world would be impoverished were it lost. Wherefore he is satisfied to live in it, and, when his time comes, to die in it. It is enough for him, and more.

CHAPTER SEVEN

SIKHISM

TRILOCHAN SINGH

The Sikh View of Religious Enlightenment

This statement is excerpted from an article by Dr. Singh in *The Sikh Review*, Sept.-Oct. 1957, pp. 30–37. It links modern Sikhism's conception of universal religion to the attempts of the founder, Guru Nanak, (15th Century) to reconcile Islam and Hinduism.

In Sikhism man is the source of religion, society is the centre of religion and God is the end of religion. The object of religion is to create a deep spiritual unity between man and man and between God and man. It helps man to discover himself and his place in the universe. It awakens him to the need of looking beyond materialistic glories and triumphs. Our conscious-self is imprisoned in the body like an oyster in a shell. When we break that ring of smoke around the self and unwrap the sheaths that cover it, we achieve here and now in the flesh the destiny of our being. Religion, therefore, is the grasp over higher spiritual consciousness just like the grasp of a musician over the infinite through the strings of his instruments. It is a growth and naturity of the best that is in man, the best that is in his heart and soul. "Religious enlightenment", point out the Gurus over and over again, "is the perfection of the whole man. Every aspect of his being must be raised to the highest point." The whole mind leaps forward and realizes in an intense moment the experience of God. The seeking, the feeling, the thinking and knowing are filled with the vision of God.

A truly religious man, no matter to which religion he belongs, is one who has attained the vision of God and who has apprehended the supreme Being. His powers which have hitherto been bound up with narrow pursuits are liberated for larger ends. The mere label or the adoption of the forms and symbols of a religion can neither make him religious nor can it take him nearer God.

"Who will be the most acceptable in the eyes of God: Hindu, Sikh or Muslims?" asked a disciple.

"None by mere name," said the Master, "Only those who lead a virtuous life and those who inwardly love God shall be saved. They would be the most acceptable to God no matter to which religion they belong."

Guru Nanak believed in the religion of man. He never gave any particular name to the religion he founded. He gave new definitions to old creeds like Hinduism, Islam, Sufism, Vaishnavism. To every old conception he gave new meaning, a new significance, because his emphasis was on the religion of man.

Bhai Gurdas, the great mystic philosopher, also points out, "Guru Nanak removed all barriers among religions and gave humanity the Religion of Man."

"The King and the beggar partook of his love, and stood equal in faith, freedom and fraternity of love. Nanak, the great one, touched the feet of the lowliest of the low, because he saw his God in every humble toiler of earth. Such was his humility and so thrilling was his message of love. Strange was Nanak's art of initiating people into his religion of love. The Master bowed to those who fed on His light. The Guru worshipped every spark of the light of God manifest in man." (Var 1, pauri 23)

Creativeness takes place both in struggle and contemplation. It is improper to separate one from the other. Man is called upon to struggle and to manifest his creative power and thus wins a stately place in nature and the cosmos. He is called to the mystic contemplation of life.

The message of Guru Nanak was not to flee from the world but to avoid being entangled and led captive by purely worldly interests. Religion, he says, should call for active exercise of will. It should inspire men to overcome the world through the power of the spirit and the might of faith. It should make the things of the earth the stepping-stones by which the soul mounts upward to its supra-mundane goal.

The Sikh Gurus made an all-out attempt to drive out from their conception of religion the following five elements which have been responsible for countless evils in our moral and spiritual life: (1) Asceticism; (2) Idolatry; (3) Varnasrama-A social order based on the caste system; (4) World-negation attitude to life; (5) A Priestly Class. The Sikh Gurus revolted strongly against asceticism and all the repulsive practices connected with it.

Religion must encourage free intellectual inquiry. Guru Gobind Singh laid great stress on that. He even trained his disciples to question him wherever they felt he was wrong. Unconditional devotion is suggested where supreme enlightenment has been attained and all doubts are dispelled.

Nothing is infallible in the world. Not the civilizations not the cultures. Neither the avatars nor the temple is infallible. Infallible is the word of the great ones. The Sikhs pay homage to the great ones and not to the miraculous history of the great ones.

If Christ had been one of the Gurus of the Sikhs we would not bother in the least about the virgin birth or other credible or incredible stories connected with his life. The Sermon on the Mount and his great examples and utterance would mean everything to us. They are sufficient to give us a vision of Jesus, the divinest of the divine ones and of God.

> "The sun shall pass away and the moon
>   And all shall pass away,
>   But ever abideth the Word of the
>   Emancipated Ones."
>
>   Guru Granth

To deprive religion of the spirit of criticism is extremely harmful. We cannot cure the mind by killing it. Mechanical orthodoxy breeds intolerance, bitterness and all that true religion seeks to abolish.

The object of all true religions is to attain the exalted consciousness of oneness with God. The soul of a religious man does not stop at an ecstasy. Ecstasy is only a station where the engine is still under steam. The union must be final and total. Gone is then the separation between him who loves and Him who is loved. Gone is the distance between thought and the object of thought. The Guru calls such a man gurmukh – Enlightened One. Nothing remains to distinguish such a man outwardly from the men about him. In this elevation he feels no pride. On the contrary, great is his humility. In the midst of his active work, his incessant spiritual creation, joy and grace enfold him.

CHAPTER EIGHT

ZOROASTRIANISM

K. D. IRANI

Zoroastrianism and the Relation of Ghebers and Parsis to Other Religions

Professor Irani of the City College of New York comes from an old Parsi family and is directly acquainted with the religious attitudes of modern Zoroastrians (the Ghebers of Iran and the Parsis in India). Though Zoroastrianism was at one time the state religion of Iran, it has become, since the invasion of Iran by the Muslims, the faith of religious minorities. The Gathas (verses) of the ancient prophet Zarathustra survive only in part as the sacred literature of modern Zoroastrian communities.

A religious conception not only interprets nature but draws from the interpretation principles for the guidance of human life. In other words, a religious conception is usually a fusion of a cosmology or a metaphysics with a system of ethical principles. In Zoroastrianism, the world in its dynamic or historical aspect is viewed as a conflict of morally opposed forces. This interpretation is itself an ethical perspective and enables Zoroastrianism to explain the existence of evil.

The essential core of the Zoroastrian religious conception is its ethical interpretation of nature and history. God created the world and caused it to evolve and progress in accordance with a principle – the principle of Right. This principle may be considered as a kind of natural law, the physical manifestation of which is light and its exemplification in the moral domain is the principle of truth. It is declared, however, that the smooth progress or evolution of the universe in accordance with this principle was frustrated by destructive forces – the forces of darkness and falsehood. These forces are personified in Angra-Mainyu, the equivalent of Satan, the original source of all evil. Angra-Mainyu is in opposition to Spenta-Mainyu, the spirit which moves towards the fulfilment of good in the universe. These two personified principles of good and evil (Spenta-Mainyu and Angra-Mainyu respectively) permeate everything and are involved in constant struggle. In the end, nature is destined to be perfected in keeping with divine purpose, but what we encounter in the temporal development of nature, i.e. history, is a conflict of opposing forces struggling for the fulfilment of the plan of cosmic evolution against its frustration, for harmony against disharmony, for progress against regress, for truth against falsehood.

Since by the very fact of existence, every man is involved in the cosmic struggle, there is no standing back. Every action or decision has a moral significance as it has some implication in nature or society affecting the outcome of the struggle. It is not difficult to see how a person is required to choose and act: one must enlist in the cause of the fulfilment of the principle of Right, i.e. strive for the promotion of good and the diminution of evil. It is an oft-repeated injunction of Zoroastrianism: Good thoughts, good words, and good deeds! Through the transformation of oneself to a state where all intentions are good and through unrelenting efforts to put all good intentions into practice, the righteous man attains his purpose in creation. For the righteous man prays: "May I be like those who bring the world toward perfection."

At its inception Zoroastrianism spread widely in Iran and its influence spread far beyond, both to the West and the East, but over the last ten centuries it has been absolutely non-proselytizing. And though some of its concepts have seeped into other religions, Zoroastrianism itself exercises little influence in the world today. The fact that one cannot be converted into the Zoroastrian community, but must be born into it, is partly responsible for the limited number of its adherents. There is an important reason why conversion is not significant: since its message of social ethics, its injunction to work unceasingly for universal betterment speaks to all, he who has taken this message to heart is in a really important sense of the word, a Zoroastrian. Of course, he does not become part of the community related by the ceremonials and the association around the fire-temple, but those are the social concomitants of religion rather than parts of its essential content.

Zoroastrianism is in this sense remarkably tolerant. If a person lives a life of righteousness, dedicated to the good of humanity, and all living things, and resisting everything that makes for imprefection, he arrives at a state of blessedness, no matter who he is. Thus salvation is dependent on one's way of life, and what one has done toward the furtherance of good in any area of human endeavor.

This is a clear indication that the individual in Zoroastrian thought is judged ethically and not doctrinally. There cannot be a purely doctrinal or purely metaphysical heresy in Zoroastrianism. But the issue of tolerance is a more complex one. Most religions view all human beings as equal, but how do they view other religions? The frequent incapacity of

one religion to tolerate, if not appreciate another is based on the fact that
the beliefs (cosmological, metaphysical, historical, etc.) of one conflict
with the beliefs of the other. Faith or belief in a body of propositions
undoubtedly has effect on man's religious life, but too often it has been
equated with his religion. Much misunderstanding and bigotry has ensued
from this confusion. What is of significance in the life of a religious man
is the fact that his beliefs have moulded his character which manifests
itself in his interaction with the world around him. In Zoroastrianism
there is, as we have seen, such a skeletal belief – the interpretation of
nature as a continuing moral conflict. This belief has been embellished in
different periods of Zoroastrian thought generating complex myths, but
the ethical implications which constitute the core of Zoroastrianism have
always been the same. From the Zoroastrian point of view (as also with
some other religious traditions) reverence for a specific name, or veneration of some natural or supernatural deity, or commemoration of some
historic events which enter into the doctrines of a particular religion are
considered ingredients of variously inspired visions and as such not subject to criticism or debate. But a religion which, say, inspires an ethic of
fatalism or pure asceticism would be opposed, not on account of its beliefs
which constitute the metaphysical or revelatory basis, but on ethical
grounds. Thus the tolerance of Zoroastrianism concerns the symbols in
terms of which religious beliefs are expressed; it may even extend to the
nature of the beliefs themselves to the extent that the acceptance of these
beliefs does not conflict with the Zoroastrian ideal of moral character and
the supreme importance of its activistic conception of the ethical life.

PART THREE

ESSAYS IN GENERAL PRINCIPLES

ERNST BENZ

OBSTACLES TO UNDERSTANDING OTHER RELIGIONS

Professor Ernst Benz of the University of Marburg, Germany, is Director of the Klopstock Institute in Hamburg and an editor of *Zeitschrift für Religions- und Geistesgeschichte*. He is also a leader in the movement for "ecumenical" understanding among world religions. He has made close contacts with Asian religions. The following selection is a translation of parts of his report to ERANOS (1957) of a recent meeting with Asian religious institutions and leaders, in which he analyzed from both points of view the difficulties which European Christians and Asians experience in their attempts to arrive at a sympathetic understanding.

The obstacles to understanding which I wish to discuss arise not only for the European observer and student of Asian faiths but also for his Asian partners in their search for reciprocal understanding. One of the first difficulties to confront even an experienced inquirer into foreign religions is the fact that he more or less unconsciously takes his own point of view as normative for religion in general. This may be a banal statement, for the warning against this mistake is one of the most elementary rules in inter-religious research. But it is nevertheless amazing to realize how difficult it is to avoid this pitfall. The mental habits of Western Christians and their philosophical presuppositions are thoroughly conditioned by the concept of a personal God. Hence they have great difficulty in grasping the basic premises of Buddhist thought and the various expressions of Buddhist piety which are completely free of such a concept. The traditional reaction of Western philosophers and Christian theologians has been to characterize Buddhist teachings as "atheistic". This makes it very difficult for them to understand how Buddhists conceive their religious communion with a transcendent reality. It was only after repeated attempts that I found myself able to appreciate the entirely different kind of religious experience which must be at the basis of Buddhist awareness of the transcendent, and which is without any theological doctrinal presuppositions, being based rather on a particular kind of training in the art of meditation. It is the cultivation of this art of transcendental meditation that makes Buddhist doctrines intelligible, not vice versa.

A second obstacle that Christians meet in both Buddhism and Shintoism is that these religions make no distinction between creator and creature. Christian thought is so thoroughly pervaded with the idea of the absolute discontinuity between creator and creature that it is difficult logically for Christians to think without this basic norm. But this conviction is quite foreign to Buddhist and Shintoist was of thinking, for to them the idea of continuity in all being is essential. The experience of unity and the perception of continuity are not only central for their meditational disciplines but for their secular pursuits as well. Hence many things are intimately related in these cultures which are kept apart in the West; so, for example, their ideas about incarnation and deification and about man's natural place in the universe. The Western observer is frequently astonished to note how easily illustrious human beings are promoted to divine honors and are conceived as particular manifestations of divinity.

A third troublesome preconception of Christians is the great emphasis which they put upon the doctrinal aspect of religion and their taking for granted that theology must be basic. As a result, Western expositions of Buddhism and Hinduism exaggerate their doctrinal aspects. I found myself perplexed when I witnessed living Buddhism to note how little of its religious life is concerned with the teachings and how central the liturgical, ceremonial, and practical aspects are. Even the recitation of the sutras, frequently chanted in a foreign tongue, is not an exercise in doctrinal learning but the enhancement of a meditative posture and mood. Such symbolical expression is unintelligible to the foreign observer, who is apt to think of it merely as an art-form. But the highly perfected use of hand and finger *mudras* or gestures connected with liturgies and religious dances, is more than art and more than symbolical communication; it is the very essence of meditation and worship, especially in the Tendai and Shingon sects. The enactment of the traditional postures of buddhas and bodhisattvas is an important aspect of the way of liberation and enlightenment and emphasises visually the continuity between the immediate and the transcendent. Even the recent Tenrikyo cult in Japan, which is not traditionalist, has already developed an elaborate liturgy of gesture and dance in which the whole congregation participates and which is more than a mere accompaniment to the chanted prayers.

A fourth point which gets in the way of the Western Christian observer is his prejudice in favor of ecclesiastical organization. But organized structure is quite contrary to the spirits of Hinduism, Buddhism, and Shinto. Their members do not build churches, and even their membership in complicated sectarian movements is not organized clearly through institutions of religious instruction. Temples and monasteries are distinguished by their varied rites rather than by any exclusive organization. Thus it is very misleading to imagine that an Oriental person must belong to one and only one religious organization. The variety of religious forms exists not merely as an historical development but as a complication in the religious individual, who may share several religions without feeling any conflict of faith or loyalty.

Lastly, the Western mind is accustomed to distinguishing religion from magic, whereas in the Orient the magical aspects of religion are everywhere evident. What the Christian regards as "demonic" is accepted in these religions as continuous with the divine. To the Western critic, with his habit of discriminating the "higher" and "lower" aspects of religion, the Hindu will explain that this diversification of religious expression does not create contradictions and confusions but facilitates the religious development of all kinds of persons and faculties. A Buddhist will take a similar point of view. Under these bewildering complications it is practically impossible for a foreigner to get a real appreciation for what these people get out of going to a temple or reciting prayers or making sacrifices before images or losing themselves in meditation. How is all this related to his basic problems and daily life? How "deep" does it go? Such questions are practically unanswerable.

II

The Oriental devotee, too, has his obstacles in trying to understand the Christian observer and his problems. The first and greatest obstacle is the traditional mistrust which he feels for the Europeans. He finds it impossible to have an open, frank meeting of minds with them. Prejudices of all sorts added to experiences of colonial days get in the way. This reticence to expose himself and his religion to foreign scrutiny should not be unintelligible. He prefers to keep these matters to himself and is suspicious of intruders. He tolerates Western attempts to understand him, but he does not imagine that the attempts can be successful, for he has a vague sense of the obstacles that bewilder the stranger. It is only recently that Europeans have showed a genuine interest in reaching a reciprocal, respectful meeting of religious minds. The condescension which goes with the traditional missionary enterprise and with colonial society has created barriers which cannot be broken quickly. For underlying any spirit of mutual understanding is the Asian's suspicion that the Christian is really interested in his conversion, or at least that he is chiefly interested in the evil aspects of other religions.

In addition, the foreigner must remember that there are many esoteric traditions in Oriental religion and that these esoteric groups isolate themselves religiously even from their own countrymen. Religion is less public than in Europe.

Lastly, with the surge of nationalism in these countries, the younger generation is apt to mix religion and politics, and to use religious media for expressing political ambitions, which a foreigner may understand more than he can appreciate.

For all these reasons and on the basis of my own experience, I question whether the time is ripe for a general, reciprocal discussion of religion between Asians and Europeans. To make such discussion rewarding there is need for an atmosphere of freedom, directness, mutual trust. And such an atmosphere is not to be found among large groups at present, though in small, intimate gatherings the discussion is already making progress.

JACQUES CUTTAT

THE MEETING OF RELIGIONS

The author, a Swiss diplomat and Catholic theologian, delivered a lecture, from which the following is extracted, before the Columbia University Seminar in Inter-religious Relations, 1957.

The very project of confronting two religions with one another seems to be based on an inadmissible pretense, and on an inner contradiction. On the one hand such confrontation, i.e. comparison with the aim of coming to a judgment, presupposes a person who puts the data "before" his intelligence, remains outside and even above that which he wants to compare. Now, of all the data of which we can become aware, the religious datum is the one which lends itself least to being thus approached "from the outside". What is true of merely human love; namely that its true nature escapes us in the measure that we consider it as spectators, is incomparably truer of the essence of every religion. Whether this essence be divine revelation, inspired vision, or primordial tradition, it is always experienced as a reality of non-human origin, as the *Sacred*. And if it be thus supra-rational, then it is not capable of being reduced to discursive examination, it is radically "unobjectifiable" and it is therefore accessible only "from within". A timeless Truth is presupposed in all religious intuition, a Truth, which, far from being posed by our judgment or depending on our choice, exists before they do, and shapes them.

But what of those who regard the different religions as so many equally valid roads leading to the same original Truth, and conceive of them as being derived from the one Truth by differentiation? Even they must recognize that this Truth, underlying all the historic religions, this immemorial Tradition common to all human beings, since it is not revealed or manifested as such, is not directly accessible, so that he who would rediscover this "lost" Word, is forced to walk the path of one of the "positive" and living religions, the only ones which can actually be practiced.

Hence, one of two things must take place: either I "observe" with detachment the mass of concrete religions in order to investigate them scientifically as so many data, in which case I am by definition incompetent, because these data are not the very essence of religions but their residues or anthropological, philosophical, psychological or historical concomitants; or else I have the required competence because my point of view is truly religious, in which case my approach to the various religions will necessarily start from one of them, namely, my own, apart from which I have neither authentic knowledge nor authentic spiritual experience.

Does this mean that the science called "Comparative Religion" is without religious bearing? *Yes*, if one reduces it to an analysis of the spiritual convergences and divergences of mankind with a view to drawing from it the "objective" synthesis, because syntheses can only be a "reconstitution" starting from a certain philosophical or metaphysical postulate, more or less conscious, and thus a simple, human, and basically nonreligious perspective. *No*, if we see in it the opportunity to deepen *our* religion.

The confrontation of religions, an ineluctable corollary of the modern confrontation of peoples and of their civilizations, is for the Christian as well as for the Hindu, for the Moslem as well as for the Buddhist or the Taoist, a providential invitation to *re-think* the tenets of his own religion in order that, in it or starting from it, he may discover greater depths, implicit dimensions or wider horizons.

In order that this may be so, one's attitude toward another religion should be phenomenological, that is, a temporary suspension of judgment, as it were, our putting judgment "into parenthesis" when facing the "thing" which manifests itself, in order that we may speak and listen. Such a phenomenological reduction does not imply that we should abandon the foundation of our own religious conditions, but only that we put into parenthesis the accidental modalities of our own religion, that is, its historical, cultural, racial, psychological concomitants, in a word, everything that prevents us from listening to the other – inasmuch as he is other – and from penetrating to the core in man where his contact with God is established. Our own religious principles, far from being abandoned, subsist as a sort of latent presence, which we shall find again, once the parentheses have been removed, enriched by new dimensions.

The Golden Rule that applies to the inter-religious relation seems to me to be the following: the more I deepen my own religion, the more I become able to understand other religions from the inside, and vice versa – the more I exert myself to grasp the other religions *ab intra*, the more I shall be led to deepen my own.

If this be the case, I think that two erroneous attitudes should be ruled out in order that the meeting of religions may be fruitful. The two extremes that inevitably menace the encounter of religions are: intolerance and syncretism.

Intolerance: To exclude at the first outset any other religion, or to mutilate it in order to reduce it to a secondary aspect of one's own religion, must be ruled out because this attitude renders any meeting impossible. In order for an encounter to take place, two persons are required, two persons who look at one another with respect. The error inherent in any intolerant fanaticism consists not in judging my religion to be superior to others, but in being spiritually blind to what actually takes place between God and the soul of the faithful of another religion. The fanatic is in fact indifferent to the spiritual destiny of his distant neighbor, probably for the very reason that he is indifferent to the destiny of his immediate neighbor. Hence, fanaticism is an extreme which falls under the law governing all extremes, namely that it sooner or later meets its opposite extreme, tolerationism.

Tolerationism rests in the majority of cases *not* on the love of man, as it believes or pretends, but rather on a radical indifference to the distinction between spiritual truth and spiritual error. Tolerationism may even be said to imply a certain contempt for religion as such. If a man tells me he tolerates me, I can hardly consider him to be a friend. As Goethe says: "In fact, tolerance should be only a passing attitude. It must lead to recognition. To tolerate means to offend." The alternative – tolerance vs. intolerance – strikes us as a wrong one. This remark leads us to speak about the other attitude that should be avoided: syncretism, which is, in fact, an aspect of tolerationism.

Syncretism, that is, the effort to combine the various religions in order to bring them to a common denominator, must be avoided because, since it claims to place itself over and above all religions as such, it is by definition, non-religious. If this be the case, religion is no longer under consideration, it has been replaced by philosophy. Now, any confrontation of religions loses its meaning if it is not religious, if it dissolves itself into a metaphysical relativism.

It is indeed true that "the consciousness of the sacred" constitutes the common basis or foundation of all the religions. But the basis is not the summit. Between the yogi and the saint, the devotees respectively of Hinduism and Christianity, the difference is much greater than between Shivaites and Christians in general. Yet it is in just this irreducible difference, at the summit, that the "specific" essence, the true and ultimate "face" of the two religions in question appears. The same is true of every religion. Hence syncretism implies, as we have pointed out above, an impossible position which no man can take; it pretends to share the position of God himself, who alone is above all religions.

Until fairly recently, the confrontation of religions has usually oscillated between the two poles we have just described: intolerance and syncretism.

The first danger is possibly more prominent in the Occidental world, inclined, as it is, toward an exclusive individualism; the second is more menacing in the Oriental world which has the tendency to dissolve concrete oppositions into an undifferentiated unity. The correction of these two excesses seems to me to be the task of the phenomenological attitude, which implies a certain reserve, a reverent expectation before a spiritual manifestation which is infinitely respectable.

The obstacles to this reverent suspension of every premature judgment, and more particularly, the danger of the two complementary errors pointed out, seem to me to spring from the fact that it is religious systems instead of religious men that are supposed to meet. Starting abstractly from some theological aspect of this or that religion, starting from one's own theology, instead of considering one *homo religiosus* as meeting another *homo religiosus* is the chief habit that must be overcome.

The inter-religious space should not be a vacuum but a sacred space which it is incumbent on man to establish. This space can enable two religions, which are two mysteries, to be face to face, neither excluding nor absorbing one another. This is what it means to meet under God, *in conspectu Dei*. Divine will is unfathomable and always mysterious, but we can set it in motion, provided we do not prescribe what it should will, provided that it be *His* Will and not ours that we will. Nothing is more liberating than to be able to discern and follow a Will which surpasses ours infinitely. It is *His Will*, present, *hic et nunc*, which liberates man, and not the futurist dream of a universal supra-religion made according to the image of our promethean limitations.

DANIEL JOHNSON FLEMING

A CODE OF ETHICS FOR THOSE WHO SHARE WITH OTHER FAITHS

Taken from his book, *Ways of Sharing with Other Faiths* (New York 1929) pp. 259–265. This is a revision of a Code presented for discussion at the Second Institute of Pacific Relations, Honolulu, 1927. It summarizes the principles developed by the author (for many years Professor of Missions at the Union Theological Seminary, New York) in his earlier book *Attitudes Toward Other Faiths* (New York 1926).

I. CRITERIA

The ethical criterion governing the *objective* in the touch of one religion on another is that the relation shall result in the best growth in all respects of the adherents of both. Among other things, therefore, the objective will include,

1) the forwarding of better relations and understandings between adherents of different religions so that all religions may have the fullest freedom to develop the best that is in them, on the basis of mutual understanding and respect.

2) the ability and the disposition on the part of the adherents to make increasingly discriminating, efficient decisions for themselves.

3) the development of alert, creative men and women, of discriminating minds, appreciative in an intelligent way of the best and finest in all life, even though they may not come to agree with the religion of their teachers.

The ethical criterion governing *reciprocal spirit* is that when the adherents of one religion make an aggressive approach to the adherents of another religion the former should seek to conduct themselves in such a manner as they would wish the adherents of the latter to exhibit were the situation reversed...

2) In other words, we should be careful not to contrast the ideals of one religion with the actualities of another.

3) A religion should not be judged by the conduct of those who do not attempt to live up to its declared ideals.

4) In interpreting another faith a person should use as much imaginative sympathy as he would wish another to bestow under reverse circumstances.

II. Individual Choice

Individuals should have the right voluntarily to change their religious adherence.

III. Propagation

In conformity with the given criteria systematic effort to propagate by sound methods any opinion, creed or practice which is sincerely believed to make for the enrichment of life, or to share values flowing from one's religion, should be recognized as proper. Some indication as to what is meant by sound methods is given by the following:

a) Expressing contempt for another religion, or the abuse and misrepresentation of it, or intentionally setting a light value on its attainments is wrong.

b) No man should preach his doctrine unless he is willing to receive and learn as well as to give; that is, unless he endeavors to maintain a humble and teachable spirit.

c) Attempting in uneducative ways, or by ways that do not honor personality, to undermine or overwhelm the faith of the uneducated or of those unskilled in argument among the adherents of another religion is unfair.

d) Fixing the religious decision of an adherent of another faith without helping or encouraging him to make a choice, and so as to prevent his making a free choice when he has grown older or more experienced is a particular instance of failure to respect personality.

e) While secrecy is not necessarily dishonorable, and may possibly in some cases be desirable, yet in general it should be eschewed, since anything that savors of secrecy increases tension, aggravates feeling, and leads to unfortunate misunderstandings. In particular parents should be cognizant of influences that are being brought to bear upon their minor children.

f) The use of material, medical, educational and economic means, not to secure converts, but as advantages which can be secured only on condition that the people in question listen to the giver's message, is questionable.

g) The use of material, medical, educational and economic means in such association with a religious message as to act as attractions, but so as to leave listening to the message effectively optional, is permissible.

h) Dependence on the example and fruitage arising from one's religion (e.g. the disinterested relief of human sorrow, suffering and need, and all noble, joyous and unselfish living) with the definite concern that others, seeing this as the natural expression of one's religious life, may be drawn to one's source of life and power, or for no other reason than that such kind of life is deemed by one to be highest, is proper.

i) Special privileges in behalf of the aggressive adherents of any religion should consist only of concessions freely granted by the people approached, and not wrung from them by the superior physical force of governments.

j) Indemnities for losses of life and property suffered by the aggressive adherents of any religion may be received when freely offered as a voluntary expression of the sense of human justice, but should not be claimed or forcibly collected.

IV. CONVERSION

The right of conversion, if properly conducted, from one religion to another should be granted. However,

a) The use of physical force, persecution, threats of loss, veiled coercion, or undue pressure to secure conversion is unethical.

b) The use of political, social, educational and economic inducements to conversion in such a way as to amount in practice to bribes is to be deprecated.

c) Detaching a person from one or more of the groups to which he belongs (family, caste, clan, tribe, village, religious body) under the motivation of merely increasing the number under one's religious label is unworthy (i.e. proselytization in its worst sense).

d) The proselytization of a minor without the consent of the parents is unworthy. One should be scrupulously mindful of the claims of human love.

e) In the case of adults one should make every effort not to break up the home unnecessarily...

V. CHANGE IN GROUP CUSTOMS

b) Aggressive adherents of any religion, when crossing cultural boundaries, should not fail to make a discriminating study of the culture and social customs of the group to which they go, since unwisely or unnecessarily to challenge or destroy local mores and ethical standards is wrong. Such propagandists should realize that the adoption of a new faith frequently leads to the loss of elements of indigenous culture dependent upon the old faith and hence they should accept-responsibility for such destruction and should provide new outlets where possible for old values. Consideration should be given to the possibility of maintaining continuity of belief essential to the preservation of morale by incorporating elements of value from the old faith into the new.

c) Inasmuch as it is a waste of national energy and of social inheritance not to move as far as possible along the lines of existing culture, and inasmuch as one of the main reasons for bitterness over conversion to another faith is not that new religious convictions have been acquired, but that a break in social and cultural traditions is involved; therefore, no element of the native culture should be discouraged unless it is judged to be a definite hindrance to the progress of the people concerned; and no element of a foreign culture should be encouraged unless it is judged to be of definite assistance to them.

d) The aggressive adherents of any religion should, in general, place main emphasis upon constructive phases of their faith, building first before destroying.

e) Aggressive religionists should temper their activities by a realization of the fact that sudden changes in social custom, organization or belief, are likely to work more harm than good where these changes are unduly subversive of established social controls.

f) The expression by converts of contempt for the seniors of their community as upholders of the old faith should be discouraged, because the effect on morality and social life is very great.

VI. Racial Capacity

One should attempt to dispel prevailing ideas and practices regarding relative racial capacity in so far as they assume that it has as yet been proved that one race or people is inherently superior or inferior as compared with another.

SHOKIN FURUTA

THE INTER-RELIGIOUS SIGNIFICANCE OF BUDDHISM

Professor Furuta of Hokkaido University is a generally recognized spokesman for Japanese Buddhism, but in this essay he is speaking his own personal conviction concerning an attitude toward religion in general. He is attempting the difficult task of freeing a particular tradition of its traditional dogmas, of its exclusive attitudes, and of its sectarian forms, in order to assert its enduring universal significance. He states his aim boldly as "stripping Buddhism of its qualities as one of the religions of the world." To symbolize the contrast he has in mind, Buddhism as a particular religion is spelled with a capital "B", whereas buddhism as free of all antagonisms is spelled with a small "b". This is a restatement of an article published in the Japanese periodical *Mainichi*, in which he expressed his hope that the ideological conciliation between East and West could be achieved by the characteristics of buddhism as a religion without antagonism.

The co-existence of opposing elements as they now are is becoming more and more difficult; co-existence apparently means the most severe antagonistic relations. The progress of modern science and advanced means of transportation by air are making the world smaller in time and space, but it appears impossible for us to expect an early solution of this antagonism which divides the world in two. In the case of religions, antagonism could and should be avoided from the viewpoint of the spirit of friendship which exists in every one of them. As it is, opposition among religions is inevitable, and is more profound and stronger than in other fields of human activity. The antagonism between Islam and Hinduism almost makes us believe that the harmonious co-existence of religions can never be realized.

Turning to the religious situation in Japan, we have no difficulty in finding many examples of antagonism among religions. Christianity and Buddhism, for example, although their intellectuals are not led by religious passion in openly attacking the religions they do not embrace, cannot help feeling keenly the difficulty of the harmonious co-existence of religions. Then, must we say that Buddhism too is destined, like other religions of the world, to find itself shadowed by antagonism? Buddhism is often called the religion of tolerance. Why is it so called?

Buddhism, in the history of its propagation in Japan, cannot be said to have been entirely free from antagonism, but cases of harmony are far more predominant than those of opposition. Judging from this, Buddhism has more elements of harmony than of antagonism. Therefore, the antagonism among religions is not inevitable to Buddhism. We have to say that Buddhism is indeed a religion of conciliation rather than one of antagonistic opposition.

Such elements or charcteristics of Buddhism have a great significance in the thought of the world. Considering the position of buddhism as a world religion, it can be said to have something significant to offer to a world beset with a great variety of antagonisms. I am going to advance this opinion in order to emphasize that buddhism is a religion without antagonism, and that as such it has a great significance in the thought of the world. I believe the greatest philosophical problem in the 20th century is how to achieve a reconciliation of Eastern and Western ways of thinking and here the contact of Buddhism and Christianity is relevant.

In Japan, it was in the 16th century that Buddhism came into contact with Christianity for the first time. The contact, however, was of a limited nature, due to the missionary work of Christianity, and did not present such an ideological problem as it does nowadays. Buddhism and Christianity must now conciliate each other in some way. Their contact is, of course, a part of the multi-sided contact between East and West. Christianity is about to find its way into Japan, a Buddhist country. The contact is unprecedentedly great. On the other hand, intellectuals of the West are coming to be interested in buddhism. Here again the contact will be on a large scale.

The conciliation between Buddhism and Christianity, the two most essentially different religions, is a matter of the future. There is no predicting. But judging from the elements or characteristics of buddhism, a harmonious conciliation appears to be possible.

I believe that the elements or characteristics of buddhism boil down to "buddhism without Buddhism"; in other words, to a buddhism stripped of the qualities which make it one of the particular religions of the world. The expression, "buddhism without Buddhism" may be misleading. By it, I mean that the teaching of buddhism is by its nature, not to be restricted by sectarian elements. Such buddhism is not a religion which limits its contents by opposing other religions. The real significance of buddhism lies in the fact that it is not limited by doctrines based upon sectarian elements.

We cannot find in the original teaching of buddhism any specific and fixed idea of sectarian egotism. This characteristic of buddhism is worthy

of note. In origin, buddhism is the teaching of the Buddha, the enlightened one, that teaches us the way to enlightenment. The enlightened one
is the person who has attained the truth, and this truth is not distinctive
of any one of the sects. It can be said that whatever doctrines and teachings
there are through which one can attain the truth, are contained in buddhism. If I am allowed to speak from the point of view of buddhism,
Christianity itself must be buddhism in sofar as it shows, in the end, the
way to the truth. Buddhism and Christianity have their own histories, and
I am not disregarding their historical backgrounds in saying that the two
are one. What I mean is that buddhism is devoid of elements opposed to
other religions because it denies itself as a religion by being a religion
without deity. Essentially there is nothing to be antagonistic about toward
other religions.

The word "buddhism" is a vague term. On its way to Japan, going
through India and China, Buddhism has been divided into sects due to
differences in interpreting its contents. However, despite many historical
changes, buddhism is essentially the teaching of the enlightened one on
how one can become enlightened. In this sense, it can be said that any
teaching which brings truth to light is buddhism. Opposition to other
religions owing to sectarian egotism is not possible for such buddhism.

Such a transcendent nature of buddhism is very comprehensive. It is
most clearly manifested in the words of Chinese Zen monks. Let me cite
an example. The Zen master Yun-men-wen-yen (949 A.D.) said, "Chien-
shih-chueh," in answer to a question by a priest, "What is the Buddha?"
Chien means "Dried" and *shih-chueh* a kind of dirt-scraper. Words exchanged among Zen priests are often mistakenly regarded as something
very unusual having nothing to do with common sense. Yun-men's
answer should not be understood as an effort to identify the sacred with
the filthy. What the great priest intended was the destruction of the fixed
idea of the exclusiveness of the Buddha which the disciple had expected
to find in his master's answer. Of course, the Zen master thought of the
Buddha as the enlightened one but at the same time believed that his
existence should not be a limited one. Yun-men thus expressed his view
that truly the enlightened one was illimitable and could be known by any
name. "Chien-shih-chueh" may be an extreme case, but there is no ex-
ception to what is universally inclusive. Such must have been the idea
the Zen master tried to express emphatically by that concise answer. If
Yun-men had known Christianity, he might have said, the "God of
Christianity" in answer to the question asking for a definition of the
Buddha as illimitable and therefore not opposing. Thus the Buddha is

identified by his way of thinking. What was said by this priest can have meaning only when uttered by an enlightened person. The Buddha is by nature inclusive and consequently can be identified also with Christ. In this sense, buddhism never stands in opposition to christianity.

However, I do not mean to say that although Buddha can be identified with Christ, there is no difference between Buddhism and Christianity. They are different religions. Their conciliation is not their identification. What I want to clarify is that from the point of view of buddhism without Buddhism, we can find in buddhism a passage through which the two religions can be harmoniously conciliated. In Japan, buddhism was conciliated with shinto. The conciliation, we might say, was due to what could be called the fundamental nature of buddhism without Buddhism. It can be said that buddhism must become endowed with the ability to embrace the thoughts of the world.

If Buddhism and Christianity are opposed to each other as the two great religions of the world, the antagonism between East and West will certainly be intensified in the field of religion. However, religion should be the first in man's activities to dissolve the antagonism. It is our duty to let the entire world know that buddhism is the most comprehensive religion, free from antagonism. I believe that herein lies the role of buddhism to cope with the faiths of the world.

WILLIAM ERNEST HOCKING

THREE POSTULATES FOR THE RELATIONS OF RELIGIONS

At the Jerusalem Missionary Conference in 1928 representatives of the Protestant churches engaged in an important debate on "secularism" and one of its immediate fruits was the demand for a reconsideration of the whole missionary enterprise not only in the face of secularism but more critically in the great "mission fields" where "world religions" were meeting each other as fellow-religions and were becoming increasingly concerned about a better mutual understanding. The Jerusalem Conference appointed a commission to investigate this problem of inter-religious relations in its practical and its theoretical aspects. This led to the publication in 1932 of a very important report by a Laymen's Commission from the USA and Canada under the Chairmanship of Professor W. E. Hocking of Harvard. A summary of this report was published under the title *Rethinking Missions* (New York 1932) and this summary which frankly recommended a spirit of reciprocity among religions, was widely discussed in ecclesiastical and theological circles and in subsequent missionary conferences, especially at Tambaran, Madras (1938). In defending the "uniqueness" of Christianity against the spirit of reciprocity advocated by Prof. Hocking, the leading spokesman was Dr. Hendrik Kraemer who published the influential work *The Christian Message in a Non-Christian World* (London 1938, 1948). Professor Hocking continued to be recognized leader of the "liberals" and published another defense of his point of view in 1940, *Living Religions and a World Faith*. From the point of view of an Indian Christian, Padipeddi Chenchiah contributed a critique (included in this Handbook above) of Kraemer's point of view and published it as an appendix to his book, *Rethinking Christianity in India*, Madras (1938). In view of all this discussion and serious searching of the religious conscience, Professor Hocking has restated his position as follows, under the heading, "Three Postulates for the Relations of Religions", pp. 141–49 of his book, *The Coming World Civilization* (Harpers 1956). The publishers have kindly consented to the inclusion of these pages here.

The relations between the several religions will be helped toward clarity if we observe the following forces constantly in play. We may state them as a set of postulates:

a) The true mystic will recognize the true mystic across all boundaries, and will learn from him;

b) Every man's religion must be "a" religion, having its own simplicity of essence, its organic integrity, and its historic identity;

c) To every man belongs the full truth of religion – the unlosable essences in whatever context they appear, and also their interpretation through history.

We consider each of these postulates:

a) *The true mystic will recognize the true mystic.*

It is all but fruitless to seek for criteria. There is, indeed, a broad pragmatic test, "by their fruits." The objective observer, being devoid of "the ear to hear," has to use this test, and so the state. The test is useful especially in its negative form: if the fruit is idleness, sensuality, disorder, the mysticism is fraudulent. Mass movements against a monastic life deemed parasitical and barren, as in the sweeping revolts against early Buddhism in China and in the disorders in England long ago, along the Scottish border, suggest the common human basis for this judgment. In a still broader sense, in so far as the religions of Asia have been, in fact, an opiate of the people, and have deferred the rational attack on poverty, the powerful element of mysticism in them is suspect of imperfect definition. And at the same time, this mysticism is near to its greatest service, the source of a cosmic patience and faith that has sustained the hearts of millions under a persistent privation which they, the common people, had no way to remedy. But the relevant and positive test is immediate: it lies in the spirit of the man; in his attainment of peace.

Gandhi was often invited to declare himself a Christian; he was such in spirit and effect; he consistently and kindly declined on the ground that "God had placed him in India," and he could do much for Hinduism by working from within, as indeed he did. But one day (I am told) an English churchman who had argued the subject with him came to the final question: "Have you attained peace?" When Gandhi answered, "I have peace," the reply was, "Then I have nothing more to say to you." The direct recognition by Irwin and Gandhi of the true mystic, each in the other, has been important for the peaceful character of the great turn of Indian history in 1947. But the recognition I speak of may be as well illustrated in events almost trifling and momentary.

> North of Hangchow there was in 1932 a new Taoist temple, founded by a Cantonese merchant who desired to restore Taoism to its original purity. I found there an old gardener, keeping a loving eye and hand on his

plantings; and in the entire absence of a common language had a few words with him. I knew that his plants were to him a manifestation of the Tao, whose polar factors, Yang and Yin, entered into all living things. As he spoke of them, I have seldom seen so beautiful a human face, enlighted with a sense of communing with the source of the life that was in his keeping. Through his garden-tending he was doing what Lao Tze called "returning to the root": we might call it prayer, in the sense of the Benedictine for whom *laborare est orare*.

With such recognition, wherever it occurs, there comes at least a readier disposition – perhaps a sort of mandate – to discern convergence, under wide differences of expression, in the meaning of essences and observances among different faiths.

Even the great induction of Christianity, "he that loseth his life for my sake the same shall find it," even this master precept nowhere else so radically and compactly expressed, ceases to stand alone. Indeed, as we noted, it would hardly be so persuasive an essence unless some inkling of its purport had been widely felt.

It has some kinship with the universal symbol of *renunciation as a condition of insight*, sometimes taking the physical form of austerity as a preparation for worship. In all religions, the capacity for renunciation has been honored as a sign of spiritual power; it has contributed to the influence of a Gandhi, as well as of a Francis or a Savanarola. Its root does not lie in vocal convention: wherever spiritual ambition appears, some spontaneous curbing of natural impulse occurs as an intuitively felt condition of the life-saving subordination of instinct. It is understood by Spinoza as clearly as by Augustine.

I had long supposed that Confucius, recommending a "Middle Path" as a primary moral principle, lacked an understanding of the firm radicalism of self-sacrifice, characteristic of the Christian absolutes. (And since it is only in the presence of such absolutes that any man can judge his own moral status, their relative absence from any tradition might account for a prevalent once-born-ness to which a sense of sin could seem alien.) But I have recently come on a phrase that throws light on the inner greatness of the aging master in his courageous persistence, despite repeated failure and occasional physical assault, in the effort to persuade local rulers to good government. The phrase "*Ssu ming lun*", which Wing-tsit Chan translates "Waiting for the Heavenly Mandate" may be interpreted "Accepting without complaint whatever fortune may attend the carrying-out of one's Heaven-appointed task" – many words for a brief Chinese phrase, but that is the nature of brief Chinese phrases! Mencius comments that this loyal persistence may involve death. And certainly, this danger-defying dedication of Confucius to his teaching mission, like that of Socrates, has been a potent factor in the enduring aliveness of his message. The principle of losing life to save it is there.

And I know of no other great tradition in which there is not a latent acceptance or adumbration of this principle, not yet given the place of priority that belongs to it. So far as this is the case Christianity, through its inductive power, may provide an interpretation by whose aid these approaches may be reconceived within their own context. And they, in turn, will provide for the Christian dictum a reconception in terms of breadth: the Christian will know better what his own precept means as he sees its identity under widely different conceptual auspices, such as those of the Chinese *Ming*, the Mandate of Heaven.

The intuitive recognition of mystic by mystic is thus the perceptive clue through which the formidable oppositions between the great positive religions are to some extent bridged. Their incompatibilities are reduced to their residual dimensions. The age before us will be to just that extent relieved of unreal contentions or estrangements. And few things discredit the position of organized religion in the mind of modern man so much as artificial or verbal antagonisms on the part of the one association devoted to the moral unity of mankind.

Not all incompatibilities will be thus disposed of; but this process of reduction will enable us to define the residue, and to assess their future.

b) *Every man's religion must be "a" religion, having its own simplicity of essence and its own integrity*, averse to the harboring of inwardly discordant or superfluous elements.

Since the mystic's recognition of the true mystic is limited by no conceptual boundaries, it is *prima facie* at odds with the idea that any one confession is the "Only Way" of finding God. If this be "Liberalism" it is but God's own liberalism, whose light "lighteth every man." But it cannot serve as our sole guide.

For if we thereupon say that all ways are good ways and add (as Ramakrishna inclined to do) that all ways are equally good, we fall into an Indifferentism that evades deep-going issues. And if we say that each man's religion is the right way *for him*, despite material divergencies, we adopt a Relativism equally negligent, and which has nothing to offer to a coming world order committed to a pursuit of universal truth, in religion as in science. Science itself has a sort of "Only Way" – its method: as Dewey pointed out, "There is but one sure road of access to truth - the road of patient, cooperative enquiry." Likewise the Only Way position in religion has at least the similar merit of rejecting passivity before crucial issues of truth and error, valid faith and superstition, right and wrong, if such issues exist. And they do.

The Only Way in religion has a further merit, that of intolerance toward a Syncretism which is disposed to borrow here and there what seems to be good, encouraged no doubt by the mystic's recognition, piecing together fragments of true insight from various sources to compose an eclectic whole, devoid of any principle of coherence. I do not mean that such patchwork borrowing is wrong: if something is found good, it is already yours; you cannot disown it. The way to an honest breadth must begin with such borrowing, as it were a tentative syncretism. But it must *come to unity* with whatever else you have. A man's religion must be *one thing*, in the sense of having a central essence which commands all else. Your borrowing, then, must be the beginning of a thinking process. Either that good thing you have found belongs uniquely to the religious organism from which it came – in which case you must adopt *that* unity – or it belongs to *yours* – in which case you must *reconceive* the essence of your own faith, to include that new element. You cannot live religiously within a divided house, or a house whose roof covers only part of its floor area!

This demand for integrity is intuitive as well as logical. Whether or not the priests and theologians of any faith are able to reach agreement as to what the essence of the faith is, the individual adherent, as he pronounces the sacred name or "takes refuge in the Dharma," must be able to feel himself at one in thought and spirit not only with fellow adherents but also with the saints in that tradition through the ages of its history. For this reason, a Gandhi, as much in accord with Christianity in precept and action, could not find this accord a sufficient reason for separation from Hinduism: his deeper intuitions were there – he said to me that the name "Rama" remained to him the most intimate and significant of the names of God – and he believed he could reach unity by incorporating his new insights within the body of a reinterpreted Hinduism. To achieve this, he so radically reconceived Hinduism as to call forth fierce hostility in some centers of strict Hindu orthodoxy. Finally his integrity cost him his life.

It is just this necessary insistence on inner unity that leaves us with a plurality of integral faiths. If postulate one tends to bring the religions together, postulate two tends to confirm their separate outlines. Are we then committed to an enduring plurality of religions, each aspiring to universal scope, and each held by its center to be the Only Way?

c) *To every man belongs the full truth of religion* – the unlosable essences in whatever context they appear, and their interpretation through history.

The destinies of religion in the age now arriving will not be governed chiefly by the findings of scholars or priests, but rather by what men everywhere seek as filling their need for an inner peace. To every man, the West and the East alike will naturally contribute whatever is universal in their cultures, no longer as western or eastern, but as his own. This, which already holds of the sciences, holds in principle of religion also, though what is universal in religion is made less available by the diversities we are dealing with, and their various geographical centers of diffusion. It is well to note that the plurality that results is largely illusory.

So far as the essences of precept and doctrine are concerned, the agreements which the mystics discern are *not similarities, they are identities*. Each man in following the Way of his faith is, of course, regarding the Way as universal – otherwise it would not be his faith. His religion is his private self-dedication to Being, which is one, and therewith his bond to the ideal community of mankind. Consciously or not, each one is seeking not "a" Way, but the "Only Way": just as any scientist is concerned to have not "a" truth, but The Truth, so the worshipper in whatever name will consider his way the Only Way, not as a proprietary nostrum but as The Truth indivisible and The Life, and as universal for just that reason. And conversely, whatever else in religion is universal is *ipso facto* part of it, and his own.

Thus understood, the Only Way, so far as its essence has by valid induction achieved finality, is no longer the Way that marks out one religion from all others: it is the Way *already present in all*, either explicitly or *in ovo*.

The several universal religions are already fused together, so to speak, at the top. The primary identity involved in the recognition of mystic by mystic is the essence of the religious worldview, the perception of Being as beatitude – God is, and God is One. With this final and universal truth whatever is implied in it, and that is much, is already implicitly the possession of every believer within his own faith. And as we have just seen, there is wide identity in a major essence of precept. So far, the religions of mankind – Buddhism not excluded – are already one religion. The area of this agreement-and-unity is subject to continuous enlargement by the processes of mystic recognition and reconception.

GUSTAV MENSCHING

THE UNIVERSAL MESSAGE OF WORLD RELIGION

Professor Mensching is one of the leaders of the World Ecumenical Unity Movement (see above, Part II). This movement attempts to clarify the difference between universality in religion and *a* universal religion in the syncretistic sense. This statement is translated from *Die Religionen und die Welt.* (Bonn, 1949, pp. 24-26)

The universal message of World Religion is addressed to the world at large, yet it encounters a humanity with different national characteristics. That is the reason why the message must first be de-nationalized and adapted to the spiritual environment of the various nations. The process may be imagined as follows: the great founders within various nations and their national faiths experience "truth", that is deepened knowledge of God and experience which touches the ultimate depths of universal human existence. These truths and the persons who by example realize and announce them, break through the limited norms of their own people. Truth and its founders must become norms for the whole world. But, in practice, this truth must be translated into the "language" of the people who are to be won by the truth and for the truth. Thus it happens that, as the history of religions shows, the universal truth of, for instance, Buddhism in India has a different quality from Buddhism in China, Japan and Tibet. But Christianity, too, is different in Germanic, Romanic and Far Eastern countries and nations.

There are limitations to the world conquest by world religions, surmountable and insurmountable. The surmountable limit is the national and linguistic differentiation of men. There is a possibility of surmounting this boundary through translation of the spiritual and religious content of the universal message into the "language" (here understood in its widest meaning as the spiritual concerns) of foreign nations. The insurmountable boundary lies in man himself. The universal message is directed to all, but not all who hear it understand it and receive it and embrace it. This phenomenon of unbelief has engaged all founders of religions. They interpret it differently in accordance with their basic personal point of view; Buddha saw in the failure to understand the essentials of his teachings a sign of the imperfect purification during the aeons of the incarnation process which was to lead to religious enlightenment. Jesus, on the contrary, saw in unbelief divine intent and Mohammed divine fiat. But, in whatever manner the world religions and their founders explain the fact of unbelief, it exists and can be explained scientifically (not theologically) as due to the lack of *"sensus numinis"* or the absence of religious experience or ability to recognize it.

The tendency to world conquest is present in types of religion with characteristic differences. In a pure folk religion which possesses its own gods and virtually hides them from alien nations, there exists, in fact, no tendency to win the world for itself. A folk religion is limited to its own nation and country. For this reason it naturally has no intention to win alien peoples and to urge them to serve its own gods.

The situation is different even with those folk religions which have reached their later universalistic stage of development. When the gods become universal, they no longer represent national property and the specific domain of individual peoples which guard them anxiously against strangers. Hence the history of religions demonstrates how, when such universalistic religions attempt to win the world, they, of course, fail. That was, for instance, the case with Judaism. At the time of Christ the Jewish folk religion had won over about seven per cent of the total population of the Roman Empire. But for various reasons, Judaism as a universal religion collapsed. Similar tendencies were present also among Chinese Confucians and in the Omotokyo Sect of Japanese Shintoism.

The real world religions, by necessity of their nature, have tendencies toward world conquest, although in a different manner, depending on greater emphasis on the prophetic or mystic quality of religion. Prophetic Christianity developed a great missionary propaganda, to unite members and nations of various races in the "Kingdom of God", which is not of this world. Prophetic Islam, however, had and still has not only the purely religious intention, to make Allah's dominion victorious in religious life, but also to include secular affairs in its realm. Here, indeed, world conquest in its real meaning was involved. This impulse to world conquest arises in the prophetic world religions from the exclusiveness and absolute character of its own experience of the divine. Only one and one's own God is the sovereign of the universe and offers salvation. All nations must serve him alone to be saved. This divine claim to dominion is to be realized with more or less worldly and forcible means.

The mystic world religion of Buddhism was, indeed, also engaged in missionary activity at the time of the great king Asoka (about 250 A.C.), but since mysticism represents an "inclusive" idea of God, that is since it includes alien gods in its own experience of the divine and makes them manifestations of one's own and only God, the claim to world conquest is less exclusive and unconditional – no harsh "Either-Or" – but a tolerant "Both-And".

There is a special form in those mystical religions, which, indeed, also conquered extensive regions of the world and represent this claim in their concept of God and salvation, whose peculiarity, however, requires the concealment of the truth of their doctrine of salvation and not to expose it to the uninitiated mass. Such were the Hellenistic mystery religions. They were genuine world religions, but they spread not through external propaganda, but, somehow, through "contagion", through the potent example of the faithful, which was unostentatious and unintended. The mystery religions bore the stamp of secrecy and cultivated the "*disciplina arcani*", the duty of keeping the secret. In spite of it, they spread over nations and countries and migrated far and wide. The religious idea penetrated through the medium of men possessed by it. In this way arose the type of the migrating religion...

Now the question arises as to the position of religion *towards* the world. Religion and World oppose each other. However not so that the world, as was the case in the conquest problem, is the place for the realization of religion and of its various forms of existence, but that the confrontation of Religion and the World is now of a basic theoretical character, with practical implications... This second question leads to the recognition and presentation of a whole series of typical positions of religion towards the world. Religion *exists* in the world only in its structural forms, different in their ultimate nature, as folk religion and universal religion. But the theoretical relationship *to* the world offers a greater variety. It can be shown, however, that the totality of historical ways of viewing the world, both potential and actual, is full of meaning and necessary in itself.

SWAMI NIKHILANANDA

INTER-RELIGIOUS RESPECTFULNESS

Swami Nikhilananda, the Leader of the Ramakrishna Mission in New York City, has written and spoken repeatedly on the theme of his contribution to this Handbook, of which he is an editor. As a member of the Columbia Seminar, he was outspoken in his urging that religions must learn to respect each other.

The respectful attitude of Hinduism toward other faiths follows the general pattern of the Hindu culture whose keynote is unity in diversity, as expressed in the variety of the customs, manners, food, dress, and language in India. But it also has a deeper philosophical basis. The ultimate reality, according to Vedanta, India's predominant philosophy, is Brahman, or the non-dual pure spirit, which is devoid of name, form or attributes. In the relative world, Brahman manifests itself as the Personal God in order to give support to the spiritual seekers in their struggle for the realization of truth. This personal God – our creator, preserver and saviour – is worshipped by devotees of different religions as the Father in Heaven, Allah, Siva, or Vishnu. A religion which regards ultimate reality as impersonal and transcendental, and at the same time recognizes the necessity of concrete manifestations of this reality, cannot but admit the validity of all religious ideals and show them respect. A historical religion which accepts the personal God as the ultimate reality, generally develops the doctrine of exclusive salvation. Hinduism does not accept the view of total error or total truth in the phenomenal world. Error may be termed as less true and evil as less good. Man does not move from error to truth, but from truth to truth – more correctly from lower truth to higher truth.

All organized religions are human institutions and therefore cannot be absolutely perfect. The deep spiritual experiences of the prophets have been expressed through human language and interpreted by human minds. Such interpretations are by no means infallible; they only hint at the truth. Religion is not God, but it shows the way to God. It is absurd to say that God is solely, or even chiefly, preoccupied with religion. Does he not notice the fall of a sparrow, the unfolding of a flower, the growth of a tree? No clock ever gives the correct time, the sun alone does that. As clocks should be corrected from time to time by the sun, so all religions by communion with God. It is good to have been born in a church, but one should not die in a church.

Hinduism accepts the doctrine of the divine incarnation and provides for more than one God-man. The Bhagavad Gita says that *whenever* religion declines and irreligion prevails, God assumes a human form for the chastisement of the wicked and the protection of the virtuous. No prophet is unique in the sense that he is the greatest of all. All receive their message from the one source, that is to say, God, and present it to men in forms suited to their particular needs. A good Hindu respects all God-men, in whatever religion they may be born.

The belief in the harmony of religions is a chief feature of Hinduism. One reads in the Rig-Veda: "Reality is one, sages call it by various, names." The Upanishad states: "As flowing rivers disappear in the sea, losing their names and forms, so a wise man, freed from names and forms, attains Brahman, and is greater than the great." One cannot distinguish a Hindu from a Moslem, or a Christian from a Jew, when they are absorbed in the infinite spirit. Later scriptures emphasize that all religions lead to the same goal. "Different are the paths laid down in the Vedas, in Samkhya, in Yoga, and in the Saiva and Vaishnava scriptures. Of these, some people regard one and some another as the best. Devotees follow these diverse paths, straight or crooked, according to their different tendencies. Yet, O Lord, Thou alone art the ultimate goal of men, as the ocean is the goal of all rivers." In our times, Ramakrishna (A.D. 1836–1886) practised all the dualistic and the non-dualistic disciplines of Hinduism, as well as fundamental disciplines of Christianity and Islam, and arrived at the same spiritual goal. One noticeable feature of his spiritual practices is that when he followed a particular path, he became completely absorbed in it and forgot eveything else. Thus while pursuing Islamic disciplines, he ate, dressed, and behaved like a Moslem, removed the pictures of the Hindu deities from his room, and stopped going to the Hindu temples. He thus demonstrated that a devotee of any faith need not give up his own rituals or beliefs, for he will certainly realize God with their help if he is sincere. Ramakrishna often described the different religious experiences as different melodies of music, and he condemned dogmatism. He asked people to regard their own religion as right, but forbade them to sit in judgement on other religions; for he said that one cannot understand the true nature of religions unless one understands God.

Religions have produced both good and bad results. On the one hand they have contributed greatly toward peace and progress, building hospitals and charitable institutions, and promoting art and literature; on the other hand, in the name of God men have waged war, persecuted their fellow beings, and destroyed monuments of human culture. And this is going on even today. It is indeed sad to think that there are enough religions in the world to give men the incentive to hate one another, but there is not enough of religious spirit to inspire them to love one another.

There are various causes of interreligious hostility. Political and economic motives can be detected in the Crusades, the Thirty Years' War, and the modern friction among the Hindus and Moslems, Jews and Arabs, and Catholics and Protestants. Apart from these, rituals, mythology, creeds, beliefs, and disciplines give rise to religious bigotry. It is often forgotten that rituals and mythology are attempts to present in concrete form the abstruse philosophy which is the basis of all great religions, for the understanding of the common people. Beliefs and disciplines are suited to a particular time and place. Therefore neither ritual nor mythology, neither beliefs nor disciplines, have universal application. They are absolutely needed to protect struggling aspirants, but may be discarded when one attains the vision of God – like husks, which preserve the kernel but fall off when the sprout emerges from the seed. When mythology, rituals, and creeds are emphasized at the cost of the essence, religious quarrels ensue. Religious people often fight over the empty baskets when their contents have slipped into the ditch.

All the great religions show striking agreement about certain fundamental principles. All admit the existence of a soul which is independent of the body and the sense organs, and that of God as the master and controller of nature. All religions venerate holy men and God's name. The Golden Rule, either in direct or indirect formulation, is preached by all religions, and all exhort their followers to practice the spiritual disciplines of self-control, truthfulness, prayer, faith, chastity and introspection. It is implicit in all great religions that men can, at certain moments, transcend the limitations of the senses and of reasoning based upon sense data and come face to face with God.

From very early times people have dreamt of a universal religion. Zealous leaders of certain of the great religions have claimed universality for their respective faiths and tried to impose them upon others by propaganda, bribery, persuasion, or the sword, or by a combination of all these. History, however, has shown that a universal religion cannot be created nor imposed upon others in this way. Later people tried to formulate a universal religion on an eclectic basis by gathering together the non-conflicting ethical and other elements from different faiths and eliminating those factors which give rise to friction. But this method has not met with any better success, because religion is not a product of the intellect; it is rooted in the direct experience of God. Because it is devoid of any such root, an eclectic religion withers away like a bouquet of flowers picked from different plants. Yet the dream of a universal religion persists. Where does one find it?

The universal religion already exists and need only be discovered. It is like universal brotherhood, which similarly exists but is not recognized because we cannot rise above our own national or racial prejudices and peculiarities. The existence of the universal religion is not recognized because we cling to rituals, mythology, and creeds, and ignore the basic truths. This universal religion is God-consciousness, which is the essence of all faiths – ethical or mystical or primitive. God is the thread that runs through all the pearls of the necklace – each religion being one of the pearls. Every sect, every religion, every soul – through refined mythology or stupid fetishism, ethical conduct or philosophical speculation – is struggling upward toward God and freedom. Every vision of truth that a man has had is a vision of God and of none else. The Bible, the Vedas, the Koran, are so many pages in the scripture of the universal religion; and many another page remains yet to be unfolded. The universal religion has no location in time or space, but is eternally enshrined in pure hearts. Its area is as infinite as the God it preaches. In it Krishna, Christ, Buddha, and Moses all have honoured places. In its catholicity this universal religion embraces in its infinite arms savages and civilized people, philosophers and lovers of God, active men and contemplatives. For the real universal religion is not a creed or doctrine; it is the experience of God.

How does one realize the universal religion? Let a man dive deep into the mysteries of his own faith, and, provided he is sincere and earnest, he will one day discover for himself the universal religion. Let us imagine a circle with a centre and many radii. The further we move from the centre, the greater will be the distance between one radius and another. And as we move toward the centre, the distance will narrow down. At the centre all radii meet. The radii represent the different religions, and the centre is God, the Supreme Spirit. The farther we move from God, the greater will seem the difference between one religion and another. The nearer we are to God, the closer we shall feel to other religions. In God we all meet. In order to realize the universal religion, which is God-consciousness, let us come nearer to God by following our own respective faiths, and not by jumping from one faith to another. Each religion, as far as its own devotees are concerned, is the shortest route to God. Our religious edifice should keep all its windows open so as to let fresh air from outside come in; but the wind must not be allowed to sweep the edifice off its foundation.

To be sure, there will always remain differences in the non-essentials of religions. These non-essentials are necessary at certain stages of spiritual development. There is no such thing as a pure religion. The whole phenomenon of religion is a complex machine, as it were, with intricate wheels. Let us lessen the friction, by greasing the wheels, and so try to run the machine smoothly. This can be accomplished by recognizing the necessity of variation. Truth can be expressed in a thousand ways; and each of these ways is true as far as it goes. We must not destroy other faiths, however crude they may be, nor superimpose our beliefs upon others, however enlightened they may appear. Proselytism is bad. We must take a man where he stands and give him a lift. When a so-called civilized religion destroys the beliefs and practices of a primitive people, it destroys something of their soul; a man's religion is part of his soul.

Human nature needs to be transformed. Religion, by revealing the eternal relationship between the eternal soul and the eternal God, by presenting the universe as a seamless unity, can bring about the necessary change. In the adventure of liberating the spirit from the thraldom of matter, all the great religions of the world must join forces in a united front.

SARVEPALLI RADHAKRISHNAN

RELIGION AND RELIGIONS

This statement on inter-religious relations by the President of India, noted educator and philosopher, is taken from the chapter, "The Religion of the Spirit and the World's Need," in his book, *This is My Philosophy*, (New York, 1957, Harper & Brothers). The publishers have granted permission for the inclusion of these pages in the Handbook.

Belief in exclusive claims and monopolies of religious truth has been a frequent source of pride, fanaticism and strife. The vehemence with which religions were preached and the savagery with which they were enforced are some of the disgraces of human history. Secularism and paganism point to the rivalries of religions for a proof of the futility of religion. A little less missionary ardor, a little more enlightened skepticism will do good to us all. Our attitude to other religions should be defined in the spirit of that great saying in a play of Sophocles, when Antigone says, "I was not born to share men's hatred, but their love." We must learn the basic principles of the great world religions as the essential means of promoting international understanding.

Besides, Whitehead observes that "the decay of Christianity and Buddhism as determinative influences in modern thought is partly due to the fact that each religion has unduly sheltered itself from the other. They have remained self-satisfied and unfertilized." A study of other living religions helps and enhances the appreciation of our own faith. If we adopt a wider historical view we obtain a more comprehensive vision and understanding of spiritual truth. Christians like St. Thomas Aquinas were willing to find confirmation of the truths of Christianity in the works of pagan philosophers. We live in a world which is neither Eastern nor Western, where every one of us is the heir to all civilization. The past of China, Japan and India is as much our past as is that of Israel, Greece and Rome. It is our duty and privilege to enlarge our faculties of curiosity, of understanding, and to realize the spaciousness of our common ground. No way of life is uninteresting so long as it is natural and satisfying to those who live it. We may measure true spiritual culture by the comprehension and veneration we are able to give to all forms of thought which have influenced masses of mankind. We must understand the experience of people whose thought eludes our categories. We must widen our religious perspective and obtain a world wisdom worthy of our time and place.

Religious provincialism stands in the way of a unitary world culture which is the only enduring basis for a world community. "Shall two walk together except they have agreed?" To neglect the spiritual unity of the world and underline the religious diversity would be philosophically unjustifiable, morally indefensible and socially dangerous.

The arrogant dislike of other religions has today given place to respectful incomprehension. It is time that we accustom ourselves to fresh ways of thinking and feeling. The interpenetration of obstinate cultural traditions is taking place before our eyes. If we have a sense of history, we will find that human societies are by nature unstable. They are ever on the move giving place to new ones. Mankind is still in the making. The new world society requires a new world outlook based on respect for and understanding of other cultural traditions.

The procedure suggested here provides us with a basis for inter-religious understanding and co-operation. It involves an abandonment of missionary enterprises such as they are now. The "compassing of sea and land to make one proselyte" is not possible when our ignorance of other peoples' faith is removed. The main purpose of religious education is not to train others in our way of thinking and living, not to substitute one form of belief for another, but to find out what others have been doing and help them to do it better. We are alike in need of humility and charity, of repentance and conversion, of a change of mind, of a turning round. The missionary motives are derived from the conviction of absolute superiority of our own religion and of supreme contempt for other religions. They are akin to the political motives of imperialist countries to impose their culture and civilization on the rest of the world. If missionary activities, such as they are now, are persisted in, they will become a prime factor in the spiritual impoverishment of the world. They are treason against Him who "never left himself without a witness." St. Justin said: "God is the word of whom the whole human race are partakers, and those who lived according to Reason are Christians even though accounted atheists... Socrates and Heracleitus, and of the barbarians, Abraham and many others." St. Ambrose' well-known gloss on I Corinthians 12:3, "All that is true, by whomsoever it has been said, is from the Holy Ghost," is in conformity with the ancient tradition of India on this matter. "As men approach me, so I do accept them, men on all sides follow my path" says the Bhagavadgita. "If the follower of any particular religion understood the saying of Junayd, 'The color of the water is the color of the vessel containing it,' he would not interfere with the beliefs of others, but would perceive God in every form and in every belief," says Ibn-ul-'Arabi. Our aim should be not to make converts, Christians into Buddhists or Buddhists into Christians, but enable both Buddhists and Christians to rediscover the basic principles of their own religions and live up to them.

Every religion is attempting to reformulate its faith in accordance with modern thought and criticism. Stagnant and stereotyped religions are at variance with the psychology of modern life. If, in the name of religion, we insist on teaching much that modern knowledge has proved to be untrue, large numbers will refuse to accept devitalized doctrines. Aware of this danger, religions are emphasizing the essential principles and ideals rather than the dogmatic schemes. For example, the moral and spiritual truths of Christianity, faith in the Divine Being, in the manifestation of the spiritual and moral nature of the Divine in the personality of Jesus, one of the eldest of many brothers, faith that we can receive strength and guidance by communion with the Divine, are regarded as more important than beliefs in the miraculous birth, resurrection, ascension and the return of Jesus as the judge of mankind at the end of human history. The *Report of the Commission on Christian Doctrine*, (1938, Society for Promoting Christian Knowledge) appointed by the Archbishops of Canterbury and York, made it permissible for the English Churchmen to hold and to teach the Christian faith in accordance with the verified results of modern scientific, historical, and literary criticism. Other religions are also attempting to cast off the unessentials and return to the basic truths. Whereas the principles of religions are eternal, their expressions require continual development. The living faiths of mankind carry not only the inspiration of centuries but also the encrustations of error. Religion is a "treasure in earthen vessels" (St. Paul). These vessels are capable of infinite refashioning and the treasure itself of renewed application in each succeeding age of human history. The profound intuitions of religion require to be presented in fresh terms more relevant to our own experience, to our own predicament. If religion is to recover its power, if we are to help those who are feeling their way and are longing to believe, a restatement is essential. It is a necessity of the time. "I have many things to say unto you, but ye cannot bear them now; when he, the Spirit of Truth is come, he will guide you into all truth." (John 16:12 ff) Every religion is growing under the inspiration of the Divine Spirit of Truth in order to meet the moral and spiritual ordeal of the modern mind. This process of growth is securing for our civilization a synthesis on the highest level of the forces of religion and culture and enabling their followers to cooperate as members of one great fellowship.

The world is seeking not so much a fusion of religions as a fellowship of religions, based on the realization of the foundational character of man's religious experience. William Blake says: "As all men are alike (though infinitely various) so all Religions, as all similars, have one source." The different religions may retain their individualities, their distinctive doctrines and characteristic pieties, so long as they do not impair the sense of spiritual fellowship. The light of eternity would blind us if it came full in the face. It is broken into color so that our eyes can make something of it. The different religious traditions clothe the one Reality in various images and their visions could embrace and fertilize each other so as to give mankind a many-sided perfection, the spiritual radiance of Hinduism, the faithful obedience of Judaism, the life of beauty of Greek paganism, the noble compassion of Buddhism, the vision of divine love of Christianity, and the spirit of resignation to the sovereign lord of Islam. All these represent different aspects of the inward spiritual life, projections on the intellectual plane of the ineffable experiences of the human spirit.

If religion is the awareness of our real nature in God, it makes for a union of all mankind based on communion with the Eternal. It sees in all the same vast universal need it has felt in itself. The different religions take their source in the aspiration of man toward an unseen world, though the forms in which this aspiration is couched are determined by the environment and climate of thought. The unity of religions is to be found in that which is divine or universal in them and not what is temporary and local. Where there is the spirit of truth, there is unity.

As in other matters, so in the sphere of religion, there is room for diversity and no need for discord. To claim that any one religious tradition bears unique witness to the truth and reveals the presence of the true God is inconsistent with the belief in a living God who has spoken to men "by diverse portions and diverse manners." (Epistle to the Hebrews 1:1) God is essentially self-communicative (Bhagavadgita IV,3) and is of ungrudging goodness, as Plato taught. (Timaeus 29B). There is no such thing as the faith once for all delivered to the saints. Revelation is divine-human. As God does not reveal his Being to a stone or tree, but only to men, His Revelation is attuned to the state of the human mind. The Creative Spirit is ever ready to reveal Himself to the seeking soul, provided the search is genuine and the effort intense. The authority for revelation is not an Infallible Book nor an Infallible Church, but the witness of the Inner Light. What is needed is not submission to an external authority but inward illumination, which, of course, is tested by tradition and logic. If we reflect on the matter deeply we will perceive the unity of spiritual aspiration and endeavor underlying the varied upward paths indicated in the different world faiths. The diversity in the traditional formulations tends to diminish as we climb up the scale of spiritual perfection. All the paths of ascent lead to the mountain top. This convergent tendency and the remarkable degree of agreement in the witness of those who reach the mountain top are the strongest proof of the truth of religion.

Religious life belongs to the realm of inward spiritual revelation; when exteriorized, it loses its authentic character. It is misleading to speak of different religions. We have different religious traditions which can be used for correction and enrichment. The traditions do not create the truth but clothe it in language and symbol for the help of those who do not see it themselves. They symbolize the mystery of the spirit and urge us to move from external significations, which reflect the imperfect state of our consciousness and social environment, to the 'thing' signified. The symbolic character of tradition is not to be taken for reality. These are second-hand notions which fortify and console us so long as we do not have direct experience. Our different traditions are versions in a series, part of the historical and relative world in which we live and move. If we cling to these historically-conditioned forms as if they were absolute, they will not rescue us from slavery to the momentary and the contingent. They leave us completely immersed in the relative. This does not mean that there is nothing central or absolute. The unchanging substance of religion is the evolution of man's consciousness. The traditions help to take us to the truth above all traditions and of which the traditions are imperfect, halting expressions. If we love truth as such, and not our opinions, if we desire nothing except what is true and acceptable to God, the present religious snobbery and unfriendliness will disappear. If we open ourselves up unreservedly to the inspirations of our age, we will get to the experience of the One Spirit which takes us beyond the historical formulations. Averroes, the Arab philosopher, distinguished between philosophic truth *(secundum rationem)* – *Tatvam* – and religious views *(secundum fidem)* – *Matam*. No single religion possesses truth compared with philosophic knowledge, though each religious view may claim to possess a fragment of the truth. "Yet every priest values his own creed as the fool his cap and bells." Our quarrels will cease if we know that the one truth is darkened and diversified in the different religions. If we are to remove the present disordered, divided state of the world, we have to adopt what William Law called a catholic spirit, "a communion of saints in the love of God and all goodness, which no one can learn from that which is called orthodoxy in particular churches, but is only to be had by a total dying to all worldly views, by a pure love of God and by such an unction from above as delivers the mind from all selfishness and makes it love truth and goodness with an equality of affection in every man, whether he is Christian, Jew or Gentile."

"The chief hurt of a sect is this, that it takes itself to be necessary to the truth, whereas the truth is only found when it is known to be of no sect but as free and universal as the goodness of God and as common to all names and nations as the air and light of this world."

Maitri Upanishad says: "Some contemplate one name and some another. Which of these is the best? All are eminent clues to the transcendent, immortal, unembodied Brahman; these names are to be contemplated, lauded and at last denied. For by them one rises higher and higher in these worlds; but where all comes to its end, there he attains to the Unity of the person." In the midst of the travail in which we are living, we discern the emergence of the religion of the Spirit, which will be the crown of the different religions, devoted to the perfecting of humanity in the life of the Spirit, that is, in the life of God in the soul. When God is our teacher, we come to think alike.

FLOYD H. ROSS

THE FAITHFUL AND OTHER FAITHS

The author is Professor of World Religions in the Southern California School of Theology, and also on the Faculty of the Graduate School of the Associated Colleges at Claremont, and Director of the Blaisdell Institute for Advanced Study in World Cultures and Religions at Claremont, California. This essay is a revision of a chapter in *Religion Can Help the World*, edited by Arthur Peabody and published by The World Congress of Faith, London, 1957, pp. 28–32. He is making a special study of religion in contemporary Japan, and his essay reflects a growing recognition among Western Christians, when they make contact with Oriental traditions and cultures, that something approaching religious reciprocity has become a practical necessity.

On a shrinking planet, where diversity is the rule (and where we hope it will remain the rule), every religious organization might well have study groups seeking appreciatively to understand what other religions teach. The attitude should be that of the honest inquirer, not of the evangelist or apologist. Some of the shorter Oriental classics like the Bhagavad-Gita and the Dhammapada and the Tao-Te-King should be read and discussed as thoroughly as the Bible is often treated by an intelligent minister in a Lenten series or in his midweek services. The basic human questions having to do with meaning and destiny have been grappled with for thousands of years; yet many of us have been allowed to fall into an idiomatic rut. Some of us might be awakened by the words of an Oriental poet or sage from our dogmatic slumbers where the repetition of Occidental phrases has operated to lull us to sleep or to superficial conclusions about life. Those who are quite sectarian-minded should ponder the words of King Asoka, of ancient Buddhist fame:

> "He who does reverence to his own sect while disparaging the sects of others with intent to enhance the splendour of his own, in reality by such conduct inflicts the severest injury on his own."

The attitude of those who insist that Christianity is "the only way" to salvation betrays a lack of faith and an undue reliance upon certain scriptural passages. The relevant question to ask is, "Why do such people seek certainty so inordinately?" To find certainty is to die; to accept uncertainty is to live, to grow, to be strengthened.

Our society today has a plethora of persons cursed with neurotic anxieties out of all proportion to real life situations, anxieties regarding all manner of things. The resurgence of tribalism, or nationalism, is but one more evidence of this profound disease. Many persons are trying to escape from facing the basic question of life, "Who am I?", by identifying themselves with various causes, some religious, some economic, some political. They are selling out to partial areas of integration, party, sect, class. These partial areas of integration thrive on feelings of "special chosenness" and exclusiveness. They are made up largely of persons who cannot forget "the Mayflower" in their past and are haunted by their unlived lives in the present.

In times of widespread commotion and unrest, it is natural that religions should look to their past. This is healthy insofar as the persons doing this are mindful of the necessity to incorporate insights so gained in the living present. Since the past holds us in its embrace, we need to understand it, but woe unto us if we cling to it or glory in it. Any "truths" so-called that cannot be directly appropriated in the present are of doubtful validity, so far as the fundamental integrative, growth processes are concerned. The "eternal now" is the straight way and the narrow gate into the abundant life.

Christians who call themselves orthodox tend to ignore this. They urge us to take only one segment of human history seriously, that segment culminating in the life, death and resurrection of Jesus. This emphasis was quite understandable in the earlier centuries of Christian history. The early theologians knew no other religious histories save that of the Hebrews and those writings that came to be called the "New Testament." They interpreted the meaning of their new outlook on life in the only terms they were intimately acquainted with. (That they greatly distorted many important sections of the Old Testament writings is now pretty generally admitted by Hebrew and Greek scholars of the Bible. I wonder how many of the Christian laymen have been encouraged to reread the Old Testament as a record of the background of the Jewish religion, and not just a prologue to the New Testament.)

To continue to interpret human history solely in terms of early, orthodox Christian interpretations of the Bible is no longer excusable. Let Christians make their confession of faith that for *them*, Jesus is Lord; but let them not try to legislate to Jews, Hindus and Buddhists, that Jesus must also be Lord for them.

We live in a time when increasing numbers of people are a little weary of being labelled "Jew" or "Gentile", "Negro" or "White", "Christian" or "Buddhist". That which unites us is our humanity, not our culture or our colour. Part of the curse of the modern world lies in the fact that so many of us have *not* discovered our humanity, but rather insist upon identifying ourselves unduly with fragments of ourselves. Like the Prodigal Son, once we "come to ourselves," we will start on the journey back to the source.

Members of a particular religion have made too many forthright proclamations or affirmations and then have prostrated themselves before them. But the "via affirmativa" is never so profound as the "via negativa", as some of the greatest mystical teachers have reminded us. Men need to learn how to die to their own concepts and credal conceits as new experiences make new concepts necessary.

Only as we recognize the fragmentariness of our interpretations of the meaning of life and history do we remain teachable. Every historical religion is a strange mixture of superstition, magic, credulity on the one hand, and wonder, intelligent curiosity, reverence, on the other. They have been vehicles for delivering man into further bondage whenever the former elements have predominated. They have been vehicles for delivering man from fear into true blessedness whenever the latter elements have been primary. All of us need to ask for forgiveness for our corporate trespasses and blind spots, no matter what religious tradition we happen to stand in, even as we hope our brothers in the other religious traditions will forgive us our trespasses against them. Let us honour a Moses, a Jesus, a Gautama, a Lao-tse, a Confucius; but let us not linger too long in the shadow of the wayside shrines of the past. If the spirit of these men is as eternally present as we of the faith have said, then we should not be concerned unduly over the particular robes that it may wear in differing cultures. What one man calls the "Eternal Christ" another man may call the "Eternal Buddha", and who among us is dogmatist enough to stand in judgment upon equally honest professions of personal faith?

Labels are of primary importance only to the census-taker, or to the person who subtly uses labels to libel. To all others, a label is simply an incidental handle for taking hold of a specific problem; it is not a club to be used against fellow human beings.

This is not so much a matter of *breadth* as it is of *depth*. A liberalism that skims the surface is just as pernicious as a literalism that tries to stop the life flow. If Christians, for example, ponder deeply enough upon the doctrine of the incarnation, they may begin to understand what Coventry Patmore, the Christian mystic, understood when he wrote:

> "The one secret, the greatest of all, is the doctrine of the Incarnation,
> regarded not as an historical event which occurred 2,000 years ago, but
> as an event which is renewed in the body of everyone who is in the way
> to the fulfillment of his original destiny."

If a Christian then follows this up with an attempt to understand the
profounder side of the Hindu concept of "moksha" (or Satchit-ananda)
and the Buddhist concept of nirvana, he may not be surprised to discover
that while there are genuine differences of overtones at certain points, a
similar profession is being made. Even modern psychiatric technique
implies the operation of a pervasive integrative factor, deeper than all
neuroses or neurotic symptoms. The psychiatrist may, for the time being,
allow himself to become the projected idealised image of his patient, even
as Jesus and Krishna have functioned for millions of persons. But the
wise psychiatrist knows that the time must come when his patient no
longer walks with the aid of an idealised image, however projected; the
psychiatrist works for and hopes for the time when the patient will "come
to himself" and learn to walk without his previous crutches. This "rebirth" process is not very different from what Coventry Patmore had in
mind by the ever-on-going incarnational process. For each of us must be
reborn day after day and year after year if we are to fulfil our innate
potentialities.

Meister Eckhart interpreted the incarnation in similar terms as involving the birth of God (or the Son) in the soul of man.

> "The supreme purpose of God is birth. He will not be content until his
> Son is born in us. Neither will the soul be content until the Son is born
> of it" (Sermon 12,).

Eckhart did not try to prove the truth of this by appeal to history, or
some event in Palestine. "Truth" is rather that which must be actualised
inwardly. It is experienced truth. (The Sanskrit word, *satya* (usually
translated "true") is a participal form of *sat*, which means "to be." It also
means actualised truth; not a conceptual formula. Eckhart speaks of
self-realisation as being God-realisation. And he expressed it in such a
way that a Christian, a Zen Buddhist or any honest seeker could gain
some hint of what he was driving at.

It is in this sense that we must approach the problem of deeper religious understanding. Our concepts must serve simply as stepping-
stones, or as the Buddhist would say, as fingers pointing towards the
moon. They must not be frozen into dogmas for then they become occasions of stumbling, of bickering and of exclusiveness.

The question might be asked: Is man inevitably an idolator? Does he destroy one set of idols only to rear another? In one sense, yes. But the tenacity with which we cling to our idols, or crutches, decreases to the degree that we grow in spiritual maturity. In the language of depth psychology of the Jungian school, we withdraw our projections to the degree that we outgrow them. Our neurotic symptoms wither away to the degree that our need to cling to substitutes is destroyed through insight. Man denied integration will search desperately for substitutes. Augustine and Gautama agree in recognising that confused, distracted man tries to satisfy an infinite need with finite sops. So long as man follows this more or less painful path, he accentuates his sense of alienation from the ground of his being, from God, from nirvana.

The rightness and tightness of some Christians' attitudes towards the non-Christian religions suggests to me something of the depth of such persons' feelings of "cut-offness." Feeling cut off from the ground of their own true being, they compensate for it by assuring themselves that it is the *others* who are cut off from God, from the true pathway, from the only way. Only as such a person finds release from the clutches of his anxieties, his sense of alienation, his shadow selves, through the insights that come through redemptive relationships with his deeper self and with other selves, can he move beyond his dogmatic brittleness. As John Oman put it in *Honest Religion*, fixed ideas, fixed institutions, and fixed theologies are all symptoms of a spiritual sickness. As Lao-tse put it centuries ago, one must become sick of his sickness if he wants to be cured of his sickness.

Christians have nothing to fear from a two-way educational or missionary process, though they have much to learn, even as Hindus and Buddhists have learned from contacts with Christendom. "There is no truth that does not include all truth," that is, if it be experienced deeply enough. Nor is it that we need to appreciate Semitic history less; rather we need to appreciate Oriental wisdom more in order to be wiser in reinterpreting our own heritage. We must not idealise the East or its religious concepts; but we *must* cease idealising ourselves and our own religion.

I personally do not look for the conversion of great numbers of the adherents of the other religious traditions to some form of Christian sectarianism. Overlooking the ever-present problem of "rice Christians", the major impact of Christian values upon these other peoples or cultures will be registered in a continuation of those traditions but with changed emphases. I would hope for the same thing to happen to Christianity. In any event, the process should be gradual and certainly non-coercive. We must respect the right of each person to travel at his own tempo in so far as the fabric of a society is not jeopardised. Just as we must let a child *be* a child in order that he may move through childhood to true maturity, so we must be willing to let persons be "Christians," "Buddhists," "atheists," "theists," "Moslems," "Sikhs," with the hope that each will grow toward an ever larger spiritual maturity.

No man-made synthesis or eclecticism can suffice. For what is needed is not a new "ism" with a new set of followers, but a new attitude and a deepened concern to try to raise the questions that really matter: "Who are we?" and "How may we come to ourselves?" Whatever synthesis emerges, it will be the unself-conscious by-product of a cosmic process, or if you will, of a cosmic bias towards reintegration and human reunion. To try to manufacture or blue-print a synthesis is to be guilty of the same mistake involved in trying to pursue happiness: the more you pursue it, the less of the it you genuinely possess.

If we learn to follow the negative path even to the degree that we cease clinging to our parochial differences, we may have taken the greatest stride of soul that men can ever take in any generation. The rest is not in our hands.

EDMOND PRIVAT

THE CLASH OF LOYALTIES

The author, who is Professor of English Literature at the University of Neuchatel, Switzerland, is prominent among members of the *Society of Friends*, (Quakers) as a student and critic of inter-religious relations. The following statement is taken from his lecture to *The Friends* at Edinburgh in 1948, published under the title, *The Clash of Loyalties*, by Allen, Unwin in London, 1949.

There is more charity in Eastern classical culture and fewer forts on their hills at home... Spiritually, as well as ethically, their culture can offer us some positive assistance. They are more accustomed than we are to cosmic consciousness. Sanscrit and Pali culture may contain much that we do not sympathize with, but it is immensely tolerant and turned, inwardly and outwardly, to the sense of the world's oneness. Both tolerance and unity do interest Friends to a high degree. Thus is brotherhood with the East a source of joy to them, especially when they meet there some elements akin to the Sermon on the Mount. Instead of being annoyed or jealous, they feel happy for such discoveries of kinship.

Does this mean that Christians have no contribution to make on their part? Neither a Gandhi nor a Tagore would say so. Indeed the dynamism of Christ and his sacrifice have meant much to them, and it is largely due to their influence that it has come to be accepted as an inspiration to more practical and active charity. The Ramakrishna Mission owes much to Christian dynamism in relief work and it is not shy about it...

Nothing is more misleading than to speak of a mixture or eclectic salad of religions. That which Friends have realized in their contact with the East is a possibility of fellowship in common acceptance of the inner light and silent realization of cosmic consciousness, the inner eye being open to a sense of what is universal and eternal, i.e. free from the limitations of space and time... The clash of loyalties, so tragic among nations, is still more so among religions. That is why we should always control our own ideas and be ready to criticize our own ways of thought, so that rust or dust may not gather in the corners.

DIRECTORY OF
INTERNATIONAL ORGANIZATIONS
CONCERNED WITH
INTER-RELIGIOUS RELATIONS

AHMED S. BOKHARI

UNITED NATIONS RELATIONS TO RELIGION

Ahmed S. Bokhari, Under-Secretary of the United Nations, Department of Public Information replied to the Columbia Seminar's request by a letter, which we publish in full. Embodied in his letter are extracts from the Secretary-general's description of the function and symbolism of the Meditation Room in the United Nations Building. On another occasion, Mr. Bokhari referred to the United Nations and its affiliated agencies as a "worldwide team of workers and leaders who are like windmills which grind for the welfare of man but which themselves derive energy from the winds which sweep across the skies. They are giving direction to history as well as drawing inspiration from it...... We are seeking a new comradeship, a universal fellowship, a world communion, a deeper understanding, and, if I may say so, the peace that passeth all understanding."

In elaborating some of the objectives of international, economic and social cooperation under Article 55 of the Charter, the General Assembly in 1948 adopted the Universal Declaration of Human Rights as a "common standard of achievement for all peoples and all nations." Article 18 of the Declaration states:

"Everyone has the right to freedom of thought, conscience and religion; this right includes freedom to change his religion or belief, and freedom, either alone or in community with others and in public or private, to manifest his religion or belief in teaching, practice, worship and observance." This Declaration was adopted without dissent so that the United Nations, without a dissenting vote, endorsed the right of all persons to "freedom of thought, conscience and religion."

Because of the many faiths and philosophies professed among the Member States of the United Nations, sectarian religious symbols have been strictly avoided in the design of the Headquarters of the United Nations. There is, however, a special room dedicated to "prayer or meditation" in the immediate vicinity of the General Assembly Hall which is open to the visiting public as well as members of Delegations and Secretariat. A reprint from the "United Nations Review" is enclosed which gives further information on the Meditation Room and its purpose.

You may also be interested to know that the General Assembly in 1949 adopted a resolution which states:

"Immediately after the opening of the first plenary meeting and immediately preceding the closing of the final plenary meeting of each session of the General Assembly, the President shall invite the representatives to observe one minute of silence dedicated to prayer or meditation." This custom has been observed since that time.

As the Secretary-General has said, "The United Nations stands outside – necessarily outside – all confessions, but it is, nevertheless, an instrument of faith. As such it is inspired by what unites and not by what divides the great religions of the world... In spite of their different roles in the life of the community and the peoples, the Organization and the Churches stand side by side as participants in the efforts of all men of good will, irrespective of their creed or form of worship, to establish peace on earth."

In a speech at United Nations Headquarters on April 24, 1957, Secretary General Dag Hammarskjold spoke of the significance of the Meditation Room:

"This house must have one room, one place which is dedicated to silence, dedicated to silence in the outward sense and stillness in the inner sense....

"The significance of a room is not the walls but in what is framed by the walls; that is to say, we had to create a room of stillness, a room of stillness where nothing intrudes on those who want to find stillness. In a way that was a help, because it meant that we could perhaps virtually do without symbols if, on the other hand, we achieved purity. Finally we felt that if within the framework we could achieve an absolute purity of line and color we could realize all we wanted, a room of stillness with perhaps one very simple symbol – light striking on stone. It is for that reason that in the centre of the room there is this block of iron ore, shimmering like ice in a shaft of light from above. That is the only symbol in the room – a meeting of the light of the sky and the earth.

"However, in a certain sense the symbolism goes one step further. I do not know whether there is anything elsewhere quite like the arrangement of this room with a big block of stone in its centre. The origin of the idea was one which I think you will all recognize; you will find it in many great religions; it is the altar. In this case it is an empty altar, empty not because there is no God, but empty because God is worshipped in so many forms. The stone in the centre symbolizes an altar to God of all....

"In this house, with its dynamic modern architecture, there are few things that give you the feeling of weight, solidity and permanence. In this case we wanted this massive 'altar' to give the impression of something more than temporary.

"We also had another idea which comes down to what, after all, we are trying to do here in this house – we are trying to turn swords into ploughshares, and we thought we could bless by our thoughts the very material out of which arms are made. For that reason we felt it was appropriate that the material to represent the earth on which we stand, as seen by the light of the sky, should be iron ore, the material out of which swords have been made and a material out of which homes for man are also built. It is a material which represents the very paradox of human life; the basic materials offered by God to us may be used either for construction or for destruction. This leads our thoughts to the necessity of choice between the two alternatives....

"We want to bring back our thoughts to great and simple truths, to the way in which the light of the skies gives life to the earth on which we stand – a symbol to many of us of what the light of the spirit gives to man. We want to bring back the idea of worship, devotion to something which is greater and higher than ourselves. We want to do that by the form of our "altar" in such a way as to bring to everybody's mind the fact that every single one of us is faced, in his handling of the heritage of the riches of this earth, with the choice between the ploughshare and the sword....

"After all, when we come to our deepest feelings and urgings, we have to be alone, we have to feel the sky and the earth and hear the voice that speaks within us. We were trying to create a Meditation Room where men of all kinds and from all regions of the world would have a place where each could find his God."

The following paragraphs from another speech by Mr. Hammarskjold on April 24, 1953, his initial addres as Secretary-General before the United Nations General Assembly, summarize his conception of the significance of religious forces in the work for peace:

"A war to be fought in the hearts of men can be waged only by those speaking directly to men. It is here that I see the great, the overwhelming task of the churches and of all men of good will of every creed in the work for peace. Their vital contribution to this work is to fight for an ever wider recognition of their own ideals of justice and truth.

"However, they also have the power to show men the strength – so necessary in our world of today – that follows from the courage to meet others with trust. We have seen how out of present day conflicts and the underlying tensions has grown a widespread state of fear and frustration, of distrust and desperation. This is, we all know, in itself a source of evil. It maintains an atmosphere in which unbalanced reactions may suddenly release the explosive power of the forces which we have to master. In the face of this development, we have reason to remember the truth that he who fears God will no longer fear men.

"In speaking for justice, truth and trust in public affairs, the churches may be a decisive force for good in international and national political life, without assuming a political role or trying directly to influence political decisions..."

SIR FRANCIS YOUNGHUSBAND

THE WORLD CONGRESS OF FAITHS

The author was the founder, several decades ago, of *World Congress of Faiths*, a fellowship with headquarters in London & Oxford, which, under the leadership of the Rev. Mr. Arthur Peabody, is still growing and organizing important discussions on inter-religious relations. Because of its basic significance for the program of *World Congress of Faiths*, the following selection is taken from the founder's reflections on the Congress of Faiths held in London in 1936. (Published under the title *A Venture of Faith*, N. Y., 1937, pp. 264–274)

The main conclusion I came to was that ultimately the basis on which fellowship, and especially world fellowship, should be founded, must be religion, but that the religion on which it must be based should be continually purified and constantly renewed. No mere ethical code, no political action, no improved economic conditions, no swifter means of communication, nor all these together, would make up for want of religion at the foundation of men's lives. But the religion which would thus be made the base of everything must be no mere priestcraft, or empty ceremonial, or conformity to conventional tradition: it must be real religion, self-acquired and profoundly felt. It should give men an acute sense of their unity with one another and with a universe which is spiritual in its nature and governed for good. Faith in the goodness of things should be the bedrock of their lives – the inner spring from which every action is impelled.

But if religion is to be the deep fountain-source of our whole life activity, it must be of our own making. We must satisfy ourselves of its truth. And we must go on re-making it all through our lives, year after year deepening, reforming, amplifying, enriching it.

We shall have to make our lives conform to the greater conception of the world which is now emerging. As we the better realize the greatness of the universe, not only in physical bulk but in spiritual quality, we shall be longing to adjust our lives the better to it and align ourselves the closer with its central purpose. We shall want something more than the skin-deep knowledge of the universe that the physical sciences give. We shall want the intuitive understanding of essentials which the organ of the soul alone can reach.

This will mean that we shall have to amplify our religion to meet expanding requirements. We shall need greater religion. Not *a* greater religion. Not any *new* religion. But greater Christianity, greater Hinduism, greater Islam....

I believe that it is such greater religion that men not only need but long for. The faintest inkling that it is in sight sets them aglow. It is the only thing that will really satisfy and make them happy. But, as it seems to me, each religion must build up on its own natural foundation. It must strike its roots down deeper into the soil from which it springs, reach up higher into the air and sunshine which surround it, so that it may blossom out in fullest radiance. The soil into which all religions strike is the same; it is the soil of Mother Earth. And all derive their warmth and light from the same source – the sun. But Mother Earth herself was once part of the glowing sun. Only the climates differ. Here the climate is temperate and religion flowers as a rose; there it is humid and hot and religion flowers as an orchid; elsewhere again it is dry and burning, and religion develops like a hardy shrub, beautiful in its plain simplicity. Each has its own attractive power and fulfils its own purpose. And all contribute to the beauty on the face of Mother Earth.

I have in me an ineradicable streak of loyalty to my native religion and like to consider myself a Christian. In the life of Christ there is a sense of humanity, of compassion, of joy and gladness, of peace and good-will towards men which endears it to me. Also, the concrete embodiments of this spirit greatly impress me. First and foremost the lives of my own dear father and mother; then saintly souls one meets who are the very embodiment of holiness, missionaries dedicating their whole lives to propagating the Gospel, parish priests giving themselves completely to work in the slums, workers in hospitals and schools all striving to elevate the lowest and bring health and light to the bodies and souls of men. These, and the work that has been and is being done in liberating slaves and, in general, improving the lot of the under-dog, greatly impress me, and will prevent me ever wanting to be anything else but a Christian.

But this loyalty to Christianity is strained almost to breaking point by the air of superiority so often adopted by Christian leaders in their attitude towards men of other religions, as when I hear the Head of one of the great branches of the Christian Church insisting that Christianity is the *only* religion for India, China and Africa; when after stating that Western civilisation is dissolving ancient religion in India, destroying the past and all inherited customs and beliefs, he declares that to survive and control the shock a religion must be found and that religion can only be found in Christianity; when, on reviewing the position in China, he says, that the only religion which could survive the shock of dissolution and hold its own in a new China is Christianity – when he insists in this way on Christianity being the only religion which can revive India and China. For in India, at least, I have seen both Hinduism and Islam reforming themselves. And I know that leading Hindus and Muslims are just as much impressed by the failure of Christianity in Europe during the last twenty years as any Christian is by the failure of Hinduism or Islam in India. The essential spirit of Jesus as it arose and spread in Palestine nineteen centuries ago must and will spread all over the world; but that all Indians and Chinese should become Roman Catholic Christians or Church of England Christians is, I should say, neither likely nor desirable. I believe, indeed, that any Pope of Rome or any Archbishop of Canterbury would find inspiration from a Hindu like Ramakrishna or a Muslim like the Bab. And Christians might well reflect that God must always have been working and must always be working in non-Christians as well as in Christians, and that it is ultimately to God that all men's eyes should be directed.

This is all the more necessary because it has been said of Christians that they are apt to make Jesus hide God instead of revealing Him. They bring Jesus so prominently into the foreground that God cannot be seen. This I believe to be a great impediment in the way of our entering into the spirit of God and a hindrance in the way of non-Christians approaching us. Whereas if what we know of the life and character of Jesus were made use of as a means to that nearer understanding of God for which Christians and non-Christians alike are striving, we and they would inevitably draw together.

What, then, is the position? Jesus was the very embodiment of the essential spirit of the universe – the very incarnation of God. In him was revealed the real character of God. He was a clear manifestation of the spirit of love in God. If we wanted to say what the universe was like in its fundamental nature, we should say that it was like Jesus. I have tried in my little book "The Reign of God" to make use of the life of Jesus as a means of understanding God. It is my view that at the moment which we know as his baptism by the Holy Ghost he did touch absolute perfection. He was at that instant imbued to perfection with the ultimate spirit of the universe. It entered into him and he entered into it. He was the perfect incarnation of God. And it behoves us, as his followers, to recapture that moment and impart to others what of it we may have been privileged to enjoy. We may, like Jesus, see the Divine in every single human being – see the radiant possibilities in each. And we may, like him, be filled with a great compassion for our fellows and long to bring life to them and bring it more abundantly, fill them with joy and gladness, and in company with them build up that kingdom of heaven upon earth of which a little child may be taken as pattern.

I believe that in this way we shall not detract from Christianity. We shall make it more Christian. In any case, our aim as Christians should be to raise it to the nth degree. It must penetrate deeper and aspire higher. It must appeal to men with some far more inspiring call than that Christ dies for them; men in millions have died for their country within our own times, and all of us are presumably ready to do the same. Men need, too, a more uplifting symbol than an instrument of torture. Through a deeper understanding of the spirit of Christ we shall reach a more intimate understanding and a more penetrating knowledge of the nature of God. Then we shall realise that God is much more than a Father. Father indeed He may be in the sense that He created us, but Mother also, in the sense that out of Her we were born; and far closer to us than either Father or Mother in the sense that God always remains in us and we always remain in Him, in the same way that a Frenchman, though he is born out of his Fatherland (or Motherland as he may like to style France) always has France in him, remains always in France, and always goes to the making of France.

For this reason men are much more intimately related to us than brothers are to each other. The relationship between us is more than a blood-relationship; it is a spiritual kinship. All together are animated by the Divine Spirit.

When we are thoroughly imbued with this new sense of a much more intimate relationship both with God and with man, we shall develop a more compassionate compassion. It will be agony to us that any should not be sharing not merely wealth – for that is not particularly important – but those joys of the spirit which may be obtained even out of the very heart of suffering. Life of undreamed-of abundance we shall bring, and with it the joy of angels. For our misdeeds and defaults we shall have to suffer, and suffer more acutely than by the physical torture of a crucifixion. Our good deeds will be their own reward. That reward will be seeing the kingdom of God arise not in a far-off place and at a remote time, but here upon earth and now in the present. And we shall have the satisfaction of knowing that we ourselves are helping to build it into its fabric and so forever form an integral part of it.

WORLD BROTHERHOOD

The following statement about the international organization, *World Brotherhood*, was prepared by Dr. and Mrs. William A. Shimer, Division Studies and Editorial Secretaries of the Honolulu, Hawaii, Office, where a quarterly publication, *Brotherhood*, was edited. The organization has undergone several changes since this article was written.

World Brotherhood is a private, non-governmental organization of men and women of goodwill who seek to promote understanding and co-operation among people differing in religion, race, nation, and culture throughout the world.

World Brotherhood was founded in 1950 at a conference in UNESCO House, Paris, by 150 distinguished leaders from 15 nations. Its program has now been extended into most countries of West Europe and more than a dozen nations of Asia, including the Middle East. A second quinquennial World Conference was held in Brussels, Belgium, in 1955, and a third conference met at the University of Ceylon, Peradeniya, in the summer of 1960.

World Brotherhood evolved from the educational program of The National Conference of Christians and Jews, which has served the cause of brotherhood in the United States since 1928, and from similar bodies in Canada and England. As in the United States the organization was created to combat the anti-Catholicism rampant during the bitter Al Smith campaign for the Presidency, so later the international program was to be directed first against the anti-Semitism in post-Hitlerian Europe.

Broadening its base from the Judeo-Christian milieu, *World Brotherhood* now deals with intergroup relations of all sorts and operates with the active cooperation of Buddhists, Confucianists, Hindus, Muslims, Shintoists, Sikhs, Taoists, Zoroastrians, and others. Application of methods and techniques to Asian cultures and problems was tested in the Hawaii Chapter, where the program is carried on by several hundred men and women, largely of Asian background. From Hawaii, the extension moved westward to the Far East.

The program is supported by individual and corporate gifts, by grants from foundations, and by bequests. Policy is under the general supervision of a Board of Directors of internationally-noted men and women, headed by five co-chairmen, now: Konrad Adenauer, Arthur H. Compton, Vijaya Laksmi Pandit, Carlos P. Romulo and Paul-Henri Spaak.

A quarterly publication, *Brotherhood*, is edited and distributed from Honolulu, and other printed materials and films are made available.

The World Brotherhood method for reaching the people as a whole is not through the usual membership-program procedure of most organizations. Rather, World Brotherhood seeks to mobilize existing agencies to include the study and improvement of human relations in their regular activities. In addition to the religious groups, there are four secular categories – educational institutions, community organizations, labor and management agencies, and the media of mass communication, including the fine or creative arts.

World Brotherhood emphasizes religious motivation and the cooperation of men of goodwill of all religions in seeking freedom with justice for all mankind. It promotes research among the social scientists directed toward the analysis and resolution of intergroup problems and tensions. It disseminates accurate information concerning the various religions and encourages mutual respect without working for or against doctrinal agreement or organizational union. The goal is unity in diversity.

A *National Conference* publication declares that "NCCJ enlists Protestants, Eastern Orthodox, Catholics and Jews, who, *without compromise of conscience or of their distinctive and important religious differences, work together to build better relationships among men of all religions, races and nationalities.* Its operation is civic and social, although obviously, *the roots of brotherhood which it seeks to build are in the moral law and in religious faith.*"

States a *World Brotherhood* publication: "By breaking down the barriers of prejudice, World Brotherhood teaches people how to live together as civilized neighbors – as one Family of Man. By mobilizing the moral and spiritual forces within the heart of mankind, World Brotherhood is helping to solve the urgent problems of waging Peace."

The Constitution of *World Brotherhood* organization includes the following article on "Objectives and Methods":

"1. The purpose of World Brotherhood is to promote understanding, justice, friendship, and cooperation among people differing in religion, race, nation, social status, or culture.

"2. World Brotherhood is a voluntary association of individuals who believe in a spiritual or moral interpretation of the universe and derive inspiration for their actions therefrom.

"3. The methods of World Brotherhood shall be educational in the widest sense. Its activities shall be conducted primarily in cooperation with educational, scientific, cultural, religious, civic, and economic organizations, and with media of communication.

"4. World Brotherhood does not compromise religious doctrines, does not seek any common denominator of faith, does not engage in common worship, does not adhere to the principle that one faith is as good as another, takes no position concerning the relative merits of various philosophies of life, and does not engage in political activities."

THE WORLD ECUMENICAL UNITY MOVEMENT

Cooperation Among Religions

The recognized leader of this movement is Friedrich Heiler, the author of the following statement of the principles of the movement. It is a translation of pp. 26–29 of his article, "Die Bedeutung der Religionen für den Menschheits- und Friedensgedanken", in Vol. II (1952) No. 1 of *Oecumenische Einheit*, (Muenchen – Basel), the Movement's periodical publication.

Articles by other leaders of this Movement (Ernst Benz and Gustav Mensching) will be found in Part III of this Handbook. Friedrich Heiler is a professor at the University of Marburg, Germany where for many years he has been advocating principles of religious reconciliation. He was a leader among the German dissident Roman Catholics, known as "Old Catholics."

In all the skillful and less skillful attempts to find a basis for cooperation among religions, we hear the call for humanity, the warning addressed to adherents of the various religions, to take their own religious and moral standards seriously, to help mankind which is sorely tried in all countries, possessed as it is by demonic powers, so that it may be led to a happier existence on the ways of truth, justice and love.

Western as well as Eastern philosophers of religion have raised their voices for humanity. Auguste Comte has clothed it, as the grand être, with the nimbus of divinity. Alfred Loisy, the father of Catholic modernism, the sagacious Bible critic and lonely religious fighter, has deepened Comte's thought and preached a "religion de l'humanité." During the first World War he lost his faith in a personal God, who, in the terror of the struggle and the cruelty of the so-called Christian nations, appeared to him as a continuing pagan of antiquity. Humanity became to him the highest religious ideal, not present humanity in all its depravity, but the idea of a great brotherhood of man united in awe before the divine and its norms. Later, inspired by sources of mysticism, he deepened this immanent religious ideal by turning towards the transcendental. His book: "La crise morale du temps présent et l'éducation humaine" (1937) is a passionate call for help in the face of a threatening new world catastrophy. In this book he brands the three totalitarian political regimes, Fascism, National Socialism and Bolshevism, as three variants of one and the same (fatal) error, as enemies of mankind. In the same way he evaluates all exclusive systems of religion which limit salvation to their own adherents and he adjures the public of the entire world to choose new paths. The religions of his day, including Christianity, appear to him imperfect; above them there rises for him the perfect religion, the "religion de l'humanité," the religion of limitless love. Loisy in his prophetic vision, sees only two possibilities: "The relations among nations *either* lead to endless rivalries and, because of their intensification of hatred, result in the extermination of all, *or* the one and only religion whose bond is love, will gather all nations; their quarrels and jealousies will disappear under the influence of love. Only a religion of love can prevent the ruin of mankind." Such a religion of love was for Loisy by no means merely a beautiful illusion: "Mankind is born under the law of devoted love; under this law, however imperfectly understood, imperfectly determined and imperfectly applied, mankind has grown, step by step, in spirituality and morality; through this law alone... universal brotherhood will be realized.... The conversion of mankind to the religion of love is no less possible now than was the conversion, long ago, of the Roman world to Christianity."

The adherents of the high religions need only to recall their profoundest ideas and to translate them into action – and mankind as one great brotherhood will come into being; then the danger of the never ending self-laceration and ultimate self-annihilation will be banished. Christianity among these religions would act as the "leader of the union of love" προκαθημένη τῆς ᾿αγάπης, to use the appelation which Ignatius of Antioch used of the congregation at Rome. For Christianity has, with utmost clarity, proclaimed love as both deepest divine mystery and higest moral ideal....

This love uproots the hatred of individual humans and of entire nations. One look at the Cross of the Redeemer who with outstreched arms embraces all men, must suffice to suppress hatred and all feeling of retaliation in a Christian. An Italian nobleman of the 12th century, Giovanni Gualberto, had engaged in a feud to avenge the death of a relative. He met the murderer on Good Friday, unarmed and in a narrow valley and he drew his sword for the fatal blow. When the murderer stretched out his arms, Gualberto suddenly remembered the outstretched arms of the Saviour. He put the sword into the scabbard and embraced his enemy as his brother. In the nearest church he divested himself of his weapons and dedicated himself to the Redeemer as a "Soldier of Christ." Such a feat of forgiving love is also heroism, indeed a greater act of heroism than the one which stands the test in bloody battle.

All high religions are able to recognize themselves in this Christian message of love: for all of them, to speak with Gandhi, aspire but to truth and love. All of them are united against war; they wage the holy war, the war against war. The high religions are the strongest protagonists and the safest guarantors of universal peace; at one with the greatest philosophers of mankind they teach the "conquest of hatred," as the German champion of peace, Friedrich Siegmund-Schultze has shown in his recent book. All clever political organizations, the League of Nations and the United Nations, are lifeless except in so far as the religion of love breathes a soul into them.

The high religions not only proclaim emphatically the peace of the world, they, indeed, create through their awakening and strengthening of the idea of mankind as a whole, the presupposition for a real universal peace. One cannot engage in propaganda for peace in a vacuum, apart from the fact that on many occasions political propaganda for peace has proved to be a deceitful shield for the preparation of war. No, first of all one must lay the foundation for mankind and humanity; once this is done, peace will result of itself.

But it is just at this point that the abysmal difficulty appears: The high religions as bearers of the idea of mankind and of peace have an extremely difficult position against the monstrous demonic powers which for millenia have played havoc in the political field. Their most dangerous counterparts are the totalitarian powers, in which the political demonic forces have concentrated in a shocking degree. The great problem today for the defenders of the idea of mankind and peace is this: Is it possible to overcome these powers, without the application of force, through Confession, witness, suffering and death, according to the pattern of Mahatma Gandhi, who overcame British imperialism in India through non-violent, passive resistance and who thus won freedom for his people? But Gandhi had a fair opponent who recognized ethical principles, as was clearly shown when, during his lawsuit, the British judge found words of highest ethical recognition for the accused. Moreover, Gandhi had numberless admirers and passionate defenders among the British people who frequently opposed England's imperialistic policy towards India. The totalitarian powers, however, have devised artificial methods to break just that non-violent, spiritual opposition or to render it impossible. By means of refined pharmacological and psychological methods, they are able to transform witnesses of the truth into automatons who reproduce their nefarious ideologies and thus they prevent any martyrdom from the beginning. Victory by the totalitarian powers would mean not only the annihilation of Christianity and of religions in general, but of the spirit, the disappearance of truth and love on this earth. As long as there exists any possibility of conquering this giant opponent by non-violent means, through the power of the spirit, each truly faithful person has the duty to practice passive resistance, *ahimsa*, non-violence.

Individuals in human society can be protected against criminals only through the physical weapons of the police. Similarly mankind at large can be protected in this malevolent world only through physical power against those who are out to kill the spirit and to trample upon humanity. Even the father of pacifism, the sage Laotse, did not advocate peace at any price, but affirmed the application of force for the establishment of peace and order in the world.

Humanitas, mankind as an indivisible whole, as brotherhood on this earth, and humanity, love for individuals and nations, free from egotism, envy and hatred, love limitless, and boundless, love of the near neighbour and the most remote individual, such love alone spells rescue for a generation of men which has lacerated itself in mounting dreadfulness in a thousand wars and now is writhing in fearful agonies; this alone is redemption from the disaster, from that final destruction which threatens it through the intensification of weapons of annihilation. This is the old message of the religions of the world and yet a new message for a generation which has been saturated with hatred in a thousand ways. "A new renaissance must come," says Albert Schweitzer, "much greater than the renaissance in which we stepped out of the Middle Ages, the great Renaissance in which the whole of mankind is discovered."

THE BHAMDOUN COVENANT (1954)

of

A World Fellowship of Muslims and Christians

A movement for Muslim-Christian cooperation on a world scale was inaugurated at a convocation of Muslim and Christian leaders held at Bhamdoun, Lebanon, April 22-27, 1954. About 40 leaders from world-wide Christianity and an equal number of leaders from world-wide Islam came together in that historic meeting to find whether or not Islam and Christianity shared enough beliefs and interests to join hands in confronting the problems and realizing the opportunities of our time.

In February, 1955, the executive board met in Alexandria, Egypt. It formulated a declaration, drafted a constitution and by-laws, and set up a provisional organization to serve between that date and the date of the second Convocation. It recommended that the name of the permanent organization be "The World Fellowship of Muslims and Christians." The Alexandria Declaration was based on the Report of the Findings Committee of the First Muslim-Christian Convocation.

The text of the Bhamdoun Covenant and of the Alexandria Declaration is taken from the *Handbook for Fellowships of Muslims and Christians.* Cairo, 1955, pp. 7-8, 22-23.

The Muslim-Christian Convocation at Bhamdoun believes that the fundamental conflict of our times results partly from the failure of people to avail themselves of the spiritual assets of religion. Even among those countries which have least been affected by this failure, oppression has frequently been inflicted by the powerful on the feeble, the stronger nations failing to recognize and respect the rights and aspirations of weaker nations. In this situation, we who believe in God and try to abide by His commandments must face the currents of atheism and materialism which have permeated all communities and nations.

The Convocation has emphasized that there is a large area in which fruitful cooperation can be developed between the two faiths of Islam and Christianity. We both believe in the one God. While holding strongly to our respective convictions, we believe that we can mutually collaborate in opening up effective channels for transmitting the teachings and morals of our respective faiths to our respective younger generations. Indeed we believe that there is urgent need further to explore ways of cooperation as suggested throughout the course of the Convocation.

We believe that we stand at a crossroads in the affairs of men. We have no quick solutions for our problems, and we possess no immediate means for righting wrongs. We do, however, dare to demonstrate our faith that it is the will of God that those who believe in Him should live as brothers and work one with another toward the goals for mankind which He has disclosed, prominent among which is respect for the inalienable rights of men and the protection of all mankind from exploitation and abuse.

We, therefore, in solemn Convocation assembled on this 27th day of April, Anno Domini 1954 – Sha'aban the 24th in the Hijra year of 1373 – do constitute ourselves a continuing Committee on Muslim-Christian Cooperation and do pledge that, under God, we will work unceasingly, with mutual confidence and regard for the rights of others, to promote understanding and brotherliness between the adherents of Islam and Christianity.

THE ALEXANDRIA DECLARATION

Humanity is passing through a deep crisis, and mankind is in anguish. Materialism, irreligion, and atheism are threatening the spiritual life of the world. In our historic conferences at Bhamdoun, Lebanon, and Alexandria, Egypt, representatives from two great faiths, Islam and Christianity, have met to discover the extent of the areas of agreement where we may cooperate in facing the challenges, dangers and opportunities of the present century. Materialism, irreligion and atheism are the breeding grounds for social, spiritual and moral anarchy. We believe that we must reorient our thinking and reassess our values, and inspire men again with the conviction that God is a living, active force in the world. Without the help of God, we are no more able to save the world than we were capable of creating it in the first place. Men must agree to be governed by God.

Much of what we seek to accomplish will have to be gained through the process of education. The values of our historic faiths, which have such great relevance for this moment in history, must be transmitted to the next generation in such a way that the youth of our lands will be drawn to God. The most powerful educational factor is the example set before youth by their elders. Our ancient truths must be interpreted in modern terms. Our moral precepts must be related to the problems of this day. Our faith must not only be lived in the mosque and the church, but in the home, the school, the market, and the government.

It has become increasingly clear to the representatives of Islam and

Christianity who have met in Bhamdoun and Alexandria that we are united not only by our firm belief in one God, Creator and Preserver of the world, but also in our belief that man's existence on earth is not merely an accident of nature, but is a purposeful act of the creative will of God. Large areas of agreement have been disclosed in our discussions together. It is clear that it is not sufficient in our times for us merely to unite on many basic principles. We must also unite in upholding and defending these principles in the face of dangers which confront us.

We pledge ourselves to do all within our power to further the spirit of friendship between the peoples of our respective faiths, to eradicate prejudice and misunderstanding, and to create brotherhood and mutual understanding in every possible way.

Convinced that God wants His people to live as brothers, and in the firm belief that this movement has developed under the guidance of God, let us strive to follow that guidance, secure in our faith that under His loving care, and in His name, all things are possible.

THE BLAISDELL INSTITUTE
FOR ADVANCED STUDY IN WORLD CULTURES AND
RELIGIONS
Blaisdell House, 143 E. 10th St.
Claremont, California

This Institute was incorporated under the laws of the State of California on June 18, 1956, as a nonprofit, educational corporation.

It has been observed that we are much more aware of the political and economic forces which bear upon the world's future than of the underlying religious backgrounds and spiritual motivations which influence peoples and shape our common destiny.

The plans of the Institute, as far as they are now formed, are:

1. To bring scholars of distinction to this center, for research, conference, development of mutual understanding and the inspiration of leadership.

2. To admit a limited number of graduate students.

3. To seek correlation with other similar centers of study, and to participate in coordinating and publicising the results.

While there would seem to be a place in any educational undertaking, and more particularly at a free, private center like Claremont, for a group of scholars to be committed to the exploration of human needs, aspirations and fears which have brought about varying religious expressions and philosophies, the exploration should include the study of the influence of religions on each other, seeking for that which they have in common as well as their significant differences.

This study should be carried on in full appreciation of the changes which the modern factual and scientific method has been making in historic and philosophic investigation, to the end that there may be a more assured understanding of man's aspirations and their fulfillment in ethical behavior as has always been important to truly religious men.

This Institute has come into being through the interest of a deeply concerned company of men and women, largely inspired by the late Dr. James A. Blaisdell, who expressed the mind of the group in the following:

"The long developments of history seem to have been moving slowly but consistently and inevitably to our present situation on the shores of the Pacific. Separating many centuries ago at the Euphrates, or thereabouts, two great human trends, with their already pronounced concern for religion, have traveled for ages in exactly opposite directions, east and west, around our globe. In these vastly differing experiences of the centuries, involving the impress made by great religious leaders, and in the long travail of thought, the original common human nature has been subjected to geographic, social, philosophic, and historic influences which were profoundly differentiating both in their nature and consequences."

"Now, however, these peoples with their intensely individual formulas of inter-related religion and culture, which include striking similarities as well as equally intense differences in our day, especially in the Pacific littoral, are come upon a profoundly new epoch in their history and indeed in the whole human drama. For now they are being brought face to face the world over. These differing cultures are being brought into co-existence in innumerable ways, but with special stress upon the institutions of religion in which these cultures find their most evident individualities."

"There is definite reason to believe that representatives of these differing interpretations of religion on the continents contiguous to the Pacific appear cordially ready to participate in common councils devoted to the effort to reach scholarly understanding, both of what is held in common and what is diverse. Here is not only great opportunity for more inclusive thinking but also one of the profoundest influences for world peace."

"It seems to be agreed that there is in man an inherent spiritual concern from which all religious aspiration of every nature takes its rise. Any mutual understanding must involve a more complete comprehension of essential human nature and its biology and psychology, a field in which much work must be done. Such an introduction must be followed by an interpretative understanding of the developments of these beginnings as they have been influenced by differing surroundings and racial characteristics, taking form in the various philosophies and symbols of religion. It is to be earnestly hoped, therefore, that this center may find association with other centers both in this country and abroad, especially perhaps in Asia, all of these centers contributing cooperatively to a common encyclopedia of religious knowledge, and in finding opportunity for expression in such publication as may be practicable."

CONGRESS FOR UNIVERSAL RELIGIOUS EXCHANGE

This organization was founded in 1958 by the actor, Lew Ayres, and some of his friends. Its temporary headquarters is in Los Angeles. (Mailing address: Box 49, 999, Los Angeles 49, California). The following outline of the organization's program and plans is tentative, but work towards establishing the Congress in an appropriate place and structure was begun in 1959. This statement was prepared by Lew Ayres.

CURE is a non-profit, chartered corporation dedicated to the establishment of a permanent forum of all faiths. It does *not* embrace an effort to introduce a common worship service nor to seek religious unity in matters of doctrine, dogma or creed.

The purpose is to enable representatives of the world's great religions to meet, discuss, and submit opinions upon urgent problems facing mankind in the present day; to provide an opportunity for devout men to cooperate in considering ways and means for preserving the rights of freedom of faith; to evaluate human achievements and world affairs in the light of ethical and spiritual teachings which have been the guideposts of human association through the ages; to enlarge our horizons and inspire us with a vision that may give direction and meaning to the future of civilization and mankind as a whole.

The Congress will be held in a permanent structure upon a permanently dedicated site not yet selected- possibly somewhere convenient to both Orient and Occident, such as the west coast of the U.S. or in the Hawaiian Islands.

In the face of the baffling dilemma of human relations in the present day, many persons have become negative, cynical and resigned to a pattern of escapism. As a countermeasure, bulletins of the activities and opinions of the world's spiritual leaders should be spread abroad each day to rekindle the spark of faith and inspire a mass determination that the unique value of the great spiritual traditions of mankind must be fully acknowledged and maintained. The tasks are enormous. Daily meetings are essential.

The permanent structure is necessary as a visible, tangible symbol of a steadfast resolution to find a way out of the predicament by reason, hard work and faith that things of the spirit are real. All participating organizations must have international affiliations in order to break the deadlock of national policy that primarily motivates and separates delegates to other world conferences. Such a world forum of faiths can co-operate with and assist the United Nations organization to find a pathway toward a peaceful and meaningful life for all mankind.

The Congress for Universal Religious Exchange will not be held in a temple nor upon sacred ground. There will be no effort on the part of the founders to introduce a common worship service nor to seek religious unity in the realm of doctrine, dogma or creed. While in a world forum no attempt can be made to assert the superiority of one religion over another, we deem it equally essential to avoid the inference that all religions are alike.

Regardless of the numbers of adherents, all major religions and eligible sectarian divisions should have representation in a general assembly. Beyond this, it is conceivable that a supreme council might be determined on a per capita basis. Each delegate, inspired by his own spiritual understanding will be expected to explore the problems on the agenda in the light of the ethics of his particular faith. Research shows, and most authorities agree, that there is little or no disagreement between the great religions in this sphere.

Every effort will be made to accommodate the religions without compromise of principles on their part. The issue stands that the right of freedom of faith is increasingly jeopardized. Unified action in the cause of mutual survival is visibly indicated.

At present CURE is conducting a survey to determine the responses of the various religious organizations; attempting to estimate budget requirements for individual and organizational grants; and making the projects known to the general public.

CURE is also acting as a center of communication for those interested in the idea. Assistance is being enlisted from all sources. Religious groups, service organizations and individuals are invited to offer such help as they can best afford. This includes personal time, institutional facilities, financial or simply moral support.

Erecting the permanent structure and financing the operation will involve the combined efforts of a multitude of administrators, clerical personnel, clergymen, artists, architects, engineers, craftsmen and laborers. In short, the peoples of the entire world are invited to share in the fulfillment of this idea.

UNION FOR THE STUDY OF THE GREAT RELIGIONS

The Union was founded in Oxford in 1950 by the late H. N. Spalding, Sir S. Radhakrishnan and Canon C. E. Raven. It was incorporated by a Trust Deed after Mr. Spalding's death in 1953. The Co-ordinating Committee and Area Committee for the United Kingdom consists of the following: Sir Richard Livingstone, Professor A.J. Arberry, Professor T. W. Thacker, Mr. K. J. Spalding and Canon C. E. Raven. The General Secretary is K. D. D. Henderson, Salesbury, Wiltshire, England.

The object of the Union was defined in the original Statement of Aims as being to promote ethical, philosophic and religious education and culture through the study of the great civilizations of East and West, with a view to better social and international understanding between the peoples of the world, and to their richer spiritual life.

The founders' belief was that just as European civilization achieved unity in diversity on a basis of Christianity and Hellenism, so a world culture could be built up and a world renaissance made possible if educational institutions throughout the world were reinspired by a common study of the spirit of man as reflected in his approach to God. The great cultures and religions of East and West – of the Far East, India, Islam, ancient Greece and Palestine, Slav, Latin and Nordic Europe, and North and Latin America – should be impartially studied and compared in their independence, integrity and fruitful diversity.

There are three lines of approach – through the study of religion and religions, through increase in mutual understanding among men of faith, and through the co-operation of religious leaders in combating materialism.

The Union's immediate academic aim is to further the study of religions in universities, where the student should obtain an outline knowledge of the great cultures as a whole and a more detailed knowledge of one, or of a group. His studies would be cultural rather than philological and sound translations will have to be provided where they are not already available.

A further function of the Union, if funds are available, will be to help individual scholars and writers, to encourage interchange of knowledge and personnel between existing centres of scholarship and research, and to work for the foundation of new ones. The production of scholars is indispensable for the introduction of religious studies into education at and below the university level.

The Union has a Council of eminent men in different countries. It proposes to work on a basis of local autonomy, with Area Secretaries and Committees, backed by local members of Council, working to further the general aims of the Movement in whatever manner is best suited to the Area's culture, needs and financial resources. Where organizations are already operating in the same field, the Union will keep in touch with them and avoid duplicating their work.

BIBLIOGRAPHY

Prepared by Dr. Minoru Nambara of Marburg/Lahn University, Germany

(Supplemented by Dr. Bernard Mandelbaum of The Jewish Theological Seminary and by Moses Jung.)

1. ALBRIGHT, WILLIAM F., Archeology and the Religion of Israel. Baltimore, 1942.
2. ALBRIGHT, WILLIAM F., From the Stone Age to Christianity, Baltimore, 1940.
3. APPASAMY, AIYADURAI JESUDASEN, The Christian Task in Independent India. London, 1951; 149 pp.
4. AKHILANANDA, SWAMI, Hindu View of Christ. New York, 1949; 291 pp.
5. ARCHER, JOHN CLERK, Cooperation and Conversion Among the Great Religions. Review of Religions, 1938, pp. 403–411.
6. ARCHER, JOHN CLERK, Sikhs in Relation to Hindus, Moslems, Christians and Ahmadiggas – a study in comparative religion. Princeton, 1946; 353 pp.
7. AUFHAUSER, JOHANNES BAPTISTA, Das Ringen der Mission mit den Kulturreligionen des Fernen Ostens. Eichstätt, 1926; 39 pp.
8. AUROBINDO, SRI, The Ideal of Human Unity. Pondicherry, 1950; 112 pp.
9. ABEGG, LILY, Ostasien denkt anders; Versuch einer Analyse des West-Östlichen Gegensatzes. Zuerich, 1949; 426 pp.
10. Acta Apostolicae Sedis, Pius XII, 1944; pp. 207, 210.
11. ANDRE, GEN., L'Asie menace, l'Afrique attend. Essai sur le mystique et sur l'interpretation des religions et des civilisations. Paris, 1953; 316 pp.
12. ANDRAE, TOR, Die Frage der religiösen Anlage. Religionsgeschichtlich betrachtet. Upsala, 1932; 79 pp.
13. ANESAKI, MASAHARU, Japanese Criticism and Refutations of Christianity in the Seventeenth and Eighteenth Centuries. Tokyo, 1930; 15 pp.
14. ANWANDER, ANTON, Das Prinzip des Gegensatzes in den Religionen. Wurzburg, 1937; 95 pp.
15. BAECK, LEO, The Essence of Judaism, New York, 1948.
16. BAMBERGER, BERNARD J., The Story of Judaism. New York, 1957; 477 pp.
17. BARBILLION, LOUIS, La Science d'Aujourd'hui et la Pensée traditionelle de l'Inde. 1941; pp. 329–51.
18. BARON, SALO W., A Social and Religious History of the Jews. New York, 1936.
19. BASETTI-SANI, Ginlio, Muhammad et S. François. Pour une compréhension plus chrétienne de nos frères les Musulmans. In: Neue Zeitschrift für Missionswissenschaft, 1954, pp. 180–193.
20. BAVINCK, J. H., Christus en de Mystiek van het Oosten, Kampen, 1934, 237 pp.
21. BENZ, ERNST, Der Toleranzgedanke in der Religionswissenschaft. In: Deutsche Vierteljahresschr. f. Literaturwissenschaft u. Geistesgeschichte, 1934, pp. 540–571.
22. BERNARD, HENRI, Sagesse Chinoise et Philosophie Chrétienne, Essai sur leur relations historiques. Paris, 1935, (1949), 283 pp.
23. BETHMAN, E. W., Bridge to Islam. A study of the religious forces of Islam and Christianity in the Near East. Nashville, 1950, 254 pp.
24. BEVAN, E. R. & SINGER, CHARLES, The Legacy of Israel, Oxford Univ. Press, 1927.
25. BOUQUET, ALAN COATES, Is Christianity the Final Religion? London, 1921, 350 pp.
26. BOUQUET, ALAN COATES, The Christian Religion and its Competitors today. Hulsean Lectures 1924/5. Cambridge, 1925, 162 pp.

27. BOWMAN, ARTHUR H., Christian Thought and Hindu Philosophy. 2 vols. London 1917, 384 pp; 351 pp.

28. BRIEM, EFRAIM, Buddha-Muhammed-Jesus. En bok om världsreligionernas tillblivelse, Lund, 1938, 282 pp.

29. BROWNE, LAURENCE E., Quickening Word, a theological answer to the challenge of Islam. Hulsean lectures 1954. London, 1955, 110 pp.

30. BROWNE, LAURENCE E., The Eclipse of Christianity in Asia. Cambridge, 1933, 198 pp.

31. BRUNNER EMIL, Die Christusbotschaft im Kampf mit den Religionen. Stuttgart, 1931, 20 pp.

32. BUBER, MARTIN, Israel and the World, New York 1948.

33. BUCK, OSCA MACMILLAN, Christianity tested – its significance for modern mission. New York, 1934, 275 pp.

34. BURTT, EDWIN ARTHUR, Basic Problems of Method in Harmonizing Eastern and Western Philosophy. In: Moore, Philosophy East-West, pp. 103–123.

35. CARPENTER, J. ESTLIN, Buddhism and Christianity. A Contrast and Parallel. London, 1923, 319 pp.

36. CARPENTER, JOSEPH ESTLIN, The Place of Christianity among the Religions of the World. London, 1904, 116 pp.

37. CAVE, SYDNEY, Christianity and Some Living Religions of the East. London, 1929 (1949), 221 pp.

38. CHAN, WING-TSIT, Religious Trends in Modern China. New York, 1953, 327 pp.

39. CHAN, WING-TSIT, The Unity of the East and West. In: Comparative Studies in Philosophy presented to Radhakrishnan, 1951, pp. 104–117.

40. CLEMEN, CARL, Religionsgeschichtliche Parallelen. In: Zeitschrift fuer Missionskunde und Religionswissenschaft 1918, pp. 97–103; 113–117; 130–134; 145–149.

41. COHEN, A., Everyman's Talmud, London 1934.

42. COHEN, HERMANN, Die Religion der Vernunft aus den Quellen des Judentums, 1919.

43. CONGER, GEORGE PERRIGO, Towards the Unification of the Faiths, Univ. of Calcutta, 1957, 126 pp.

44. CRAGG, KENNETH A., Each Other's Faith- some thoughts on Muslim-Christian colloquy today. In: Muslim World 1955, pp. 145–171.

45. CRANDALL, KENNETH H., The Impact of Islam on Christianity. New York, 1952, 11 pp.

46. DANIELOU, JEAN PERE, Le Problème Théologique des Religions Non-Chretiennes. In: Metafisica ed Esperienza Religiosa, Archivio di Filosofia, Organo dell' Instituto di Studi Filosofici. Roma, 1956, pp. 203–33.

47. DANIELOU, JEAN, Y a-t-il une Crise des Missions Etrangères? In: Union Missionaire du Clergé de France, Paris, 1956, pp. 226–235.

48. DAVIS, MOSHE (ed), Israel: Its Role in Civilization, New York, 1956.

49. DEVARANNE, THEODOR, Mythus und Christus im Fernen Osten. Berlin 1938, 31 pp.

50. DEWICK, EDWARD CHISHOLM, The Christian Attitude to other Religions. Cambridge, 1953, 220 pp.

51. EDGAR, LESLIE I., Cooperation between World Religions, Boston 1953, 33 pp.

52. ELBOGEN, ISMAR, Der Juedische Gottesdienst, 1931.

53. ELIADE, MIRCEA, Phenomenologie de la Religion et Sociologie Religieuse. In: Critique 1949, pp. 713–720.

54. ELWIN, VERRIER, Christian Dhyâna, or prayer of loving regard – a study of the "cloud of unknowing". London, 1930, 74 pp.

55. Encyclical RERUM ECCLESIAE of Pope Pius XI. (Norms for Catholic Missions)

56. EPSTEIN, ISIDORE, The Faith of Judaism, London 1954.

57. Eranos-Jahrbuch, Zur Gestaltung der Eloesungsidee in Ost und West. Zuerich, 1938, 353 pp.
58. Falke, Robert, Im Kampf der drei Weltreligionen. Ein Katechismus fuer wahrheitsuchende Leute. Leipzig, 1902, 102 pp.
59. Filliozat, Jean, Interprétation Occidentale de la Pensée Indienne. In: Education mars–mai 1949, pp. 1–16.
60. Finkelstein, Louis, (ed), The Jews, Their History, Culture and Religion. 4 vols. Philadelphia 1949.
61. Fleming, Daniel Johnson, Attitudes toward other Faiths. New York 1928, 166 pp.
62. Fleming, Daniel Johnson, Ways of Sharing with other Faiths. New York 1929, 268 pp.
63. Frick, Heinrich, Christliche Grundbegriffe in ihrer Besonderheit gegenüber Fremdreligionen. In: Evangel. Missionsmagazin. 1944; pp. 205–225.
64. Frick, Heinrich, Das Evangelium und die Religionen. Basel, 1933; 54 pp.
65. Gabriel, Walt, Gandhi, Christus und wir Christen. Halle a.S. 1931; 61 pp.
66. Garbe, Richard, Contributions of Christianity to Buddhism. In: The Monist, 1912; pp. 161–87.
67. George, S. K., Gandhi's Challenge to Christianity. London, 1940; 112 pp.
68. Glasenapp, Helmut von, Buddhismus und Christentum. In: Universitas 1949; pp. 1–13.
69. Goitein, Solomon D. F., Jews and Arabs – Their Contacts Through the Ages, New York, 1955.
70. Gordis, Robert, Judaism for the Modern Age, New York, 1955.
71. Grabs, Rudolf, Die Weltreligionen im Blickpunkte Albert Schweitzers. Berlin, 1953, 76 pp.
72. Haas, Hans, Buddhismus und Christentum. Bibliographie zur Frage nach den Wechselbeziehungen zwischen Buddhismus und Christentum. Berlin, 1921.
73. Haas, Hans, Tenrikyô, Ein neues synkretistisches Religionsbild im Japan unserer Tage. In: Zeitschrift für Missionskunde und Religionswissenschaft 1910; pp. 129–45.
74. Harker, F. D., Teachest Thou Thyself? A Challenge to Christian teachers. London, 1953; 112 pp.
75. Hartenstein, Karl, Die missionarische Begegnung mit dem Heidentum. Stuttgart, 1938; 16 pp.
76. Heiler, Friedrich, How can Christian and non-Christian Religions co-operate? In: The Hibbert Journal, 1954; pp. 107–118.
77. Heiler, Friedrich, Christlicher Glaube und indisches Geisteslieben. München, 1926; 104 pp.
78. Heiler, Friedrich, Die Absolutheit des Christentums im Lichte der allgemeinen Religionsgeschichte. In: Das Wesen des Katholizismus, 1920, pp. 116–137 (Eine heilige Kirche 1938, H. 11 & 12.)
68. Heiler, Friedrich, Gottesoffenbarung im Heidentum und Christentum. In: Eine heilige Kirche, 1938, Heft 11/12.
69. Heiler, Friedrich, "Mut zur Liebe"– die Zusammenarbeit der Religionen im Dienste der ganzen Menschheit. In: Eine Heilige Kirche 1953/4, pp. 18–33.
70. Heiler, Friedrich, Um die Zusammenarbeit der Christenheit mit den ausserchristlichen Religionsgemeinschaften. In: Schweizerische Theologische Umschau, 1952, pp. 1–11.
71. Herberg, Will, Judaism and Modern Man. Philadelphia 1951.
72. Herberg, Will, Protestant-Catholic-Jew, New York 1955.
73. Herbert, Jean, Yogas, Christianisme, et Civilisation. Paris, 1953, 48 pp.
74. Herford, Travers, The Pharisees, London, 1924.

75. HERTZ, JOSEPH H., The Authorized Daily Prayerbook, New York 1953.
76. HILLIARD, F. H., The Buddha, the Prophet and the Christ, New York, 1956, 169 pp.
77. HOCKING, W. E., Living Religions and a World Faith. Hibbert Lectures 1938. New York, 1940, 291 pp.
78. HOLSTEN, WALTER, Das Evangelium und die Völker. Beiträge zur Geschichte und Theorie der Mission. Berlin, 1939, 166 pp.
79. HUGHES, ERNEST RICHARD, Religion in China. London 1950, 151 pp.
80. IDELSOHN, ABRAHAM Z., Jewish Music in Its Historical Development, New York 1929.
81. IMMANUEL, RAJAPPAN, D., The Influence of Hinduism on Indian Christians, Jubbulpore, 1950, 251 pp.
82. IRWIN, WILLIAM, The Old Testament: Keystone to Human Culture, New York 1952.
83. JAGADESWARANANDA, SWAMI, A Christian misunderstands Buddhism. In: The Maha-Bodhi 1942, Numb. 4–6.
84. JOSEPH, MORRIS, Judaism as Creed and Life, New York 1920.
85. JUNG, LEO (ed.) Judaism in a Changing World, New York, 1939, 294 pp.
86. JUNG, LEO, (ed.) The Jewish Library, New York, 1928–1959.
87. JURJI, EDWARD JABRA, Christian Interpretation of Religion – Christianity in its human and creative relationships with the world's cultures and faiths. New York, 1952, 318 pp.
88. KAGAWA, TOYOHIKO, Christ and Japan. London and New York, 1934, 126 pp.
89. KARRER, OTTO, Das Religiöse in der Menschheit und das Christentum. Freiburg i. Br., 1933, 264 pp.
90. KAPLAN, MORDECAI M., The Meaning of God in Modern Jewish Religion, New York 1947.
91. KATSH, ABRAHAM I., Judaism in Islam, New York 1954.
92. KEHIMKAR, H. S., The History of the Bene-Israel of India, Tel Aviv, 1937.
93. KEILBACH, WILHELM, Die Problematik der Religionen. Religionsphilosophische Studie mit besonderer Berücksichtigung der neuen Religionspsychologie. Paderborn, 1936, 271 pp.
94. KITAGAWA, JOSEPH M., Theology and the Science of Religion. In: Anglican Theol. Rev. 1957, pp. 1–20.
95. KLAUSNER, JOSEPH, Jesus of Nazareth, New York, 1925.
96. KOHLER, KAUFMAN, Jewish Theology, New York 1918.
97. KRAEMER, HENDRIK, Religion and the Christian Faith, London, 1956, 461 pp.
98. KRAEMER, HENDRIK, Syncretism as a Religious and Missionary Problem. In: International Review of Missions 1954, pp. 253–273.
99. KRAEMER, HENDRIK, The Christian Message in a Non-Christian World. London, 1938, 454 pp.
100. LACOMBE, OLIVIER, La Pensée Catholique Traditionelle et l'Hindouisme. In: Le Monde Non-Chrétien 1951, pp. 387–401.
101. LAZARUS, MORITZ, The Ethics of Judaism, Philadelphia, 1901.
102. LEVI, SYLVAIN, L'Inde et le Monde, Paris, 1926, 175 pp.
103. LEVONIAN, LOOTFY, Moslem Mentality – a discussion of the presentation of Christianity to Moslems. London, 1928, 246 pp.
104. LIANG-SI-ING, Christ ou Confucius? La rencontre et la conflit entre les idees des missionaires chrétiens et les idees des Chinois en Chine depuis la fin de la dynastie des Ming. Paris, 1940, 159 pp.
105. LOHUIZEN, J. E. & VAN DE LEEUW, The Meeting between East and West. In: East and West, 1956, pp. 5–11.
106. LOWDERMILK, WALTER CLAY, Palestine, Land of Promise, New York 1944.

107. Lubac, Henry de, La Racontre du Bouddhisme et de l'Occident. Paris, 1952, 285 pp.
108. Macdonald, Duncan B., The Unity of the Mystical Experience in Islam and Christendom. In: Muslim World 1935, pp. 325–335.
109. Macnicol, Nicol, Is Christianity Unique? – A comparative study of the religions. London, 1936, 222 pp.
110. Macnicol, Nicol, The Living Religions of the Indian People, London 1934, 324 pp.
111. Marx, Alexander and Margolis, Max, A History of the Jewish People, Philadelphia, 1921.
112. Masson-Oursel, Paul, Foi Bouddhique et Foi Chrétienne. In: Congrès d'Histoire du Christianisme; Jubilé Alfred Loisy, Annales d'Histoire du Christianisme. Paris, 1928.
113. McKenzie, John, Two Religions. A comparative study of some distinctive ideals in Hinduism and Christianity. London, 1950, 143 pp.
115. Melzer, Friso, Christus und die indischen Erloesungswege. Tuebingen, 1949, 190 pp.
116. Mensching, Gustav, Buddha und Christus. Bonn, 1952, 409 pp.
117. Mensching Gustav, Toleranz und Wahrheit in der Religion. Heidelberg, 1955, 196 pp.
118. Merkel, Rudolf Franz, Gebete der Voelker, Muenchen 1953, 192 pp.
119. Mohammed Fosil, S., Conversion and Cooperation in Religion. Madras 1924.
120. Mohammed Iqbal, S., Reconstruire la Pensée religieuse de l'Islam. Paris, 1955, 214 pp.
121. Moore, George Foot, Judaism, Harvard Univ. Press, Cambridge 1927.
122. Morris, Charles, Comparative Strength of Life-Ideals in Eastern and Western Cultures. In: Moore, Philsophy East and West. pp. 253–270.
123. Moses, David G., Christianity and the Non-Christian Religions. In: International Review of Missions, 1954, pp. 146–154.
124. Moses, D. G., Religious Truth and the Relation between Religions, Madras, 1950.
125. Murphy, Edward I., S.J. teach ye all nations: The Principles of Catholic Missionary Work. New York.
126. Northrop, Filmer S.C., The Relation between Eastern and Western Philosophy. In: Comparative Studies in Philos. presented to Radhakrishnan, London, 1951.
127. Ohm, Thomas, Asiens Kritik am abendlandlichen Christentum. Muenchen 1948, 215 pp.
128. Ohm Thomas, Die Gebetsgebärden der Völker und das Christentum. Munster, 1948, 148 pp.
129. Ohm, Thomas, Kulturen, Religionen und Missionen in Japan. Augsburg, 1929, 216 pp.
130. Paton, William, The Syncretistic Mood in East and West. In: Student World 1934, pp. 308–314.
131. Platt, Mary S. (ed), Christ comes to the Village – a study of rural life in non-Christian lands. Cambridge, 1931, 187 pp.
132. Privat, Edmond, Sagesse de l'Orient. Au-dela des Religions, Neuchatel, 1947, 127 pp.
133. Radhakrishnan, Sarvepalli, Eastern and Western Religion. London, 1933, 146 pp.
134. Radhakrishnan, Sarvepalli, Religion and Society, London 1948, 242 pp.
135. Radhakrishnan, Sarvepalli, The Hindu View of Life. London, 1926, 133 pp.
136. Raisin, Jacob S., Gentile Reactions to Jewish Ideals, New York 1953, 876 pp.

137. RAU, MARK SANJIVA, Types of Religious Consciousness. Hindu and Christian. Mangalore, 1932, 64 pp.

138. RAVEN, CHARLES EARLE, Natural Religion and Christian Theology. The Gifford Lectures 1952. London, 1953, 227 pp.

139. RAWLINSON, FRANK, Naturalization of Christianity in China – a study of the relation of Christian and Chinese Idealism and Life. Shanghai, 1927, 216 pp.

140. REISCHAUER, A. K., Non-Christian Religions and Christian Leadership. In: International Review of Missions 1954, pp. 179–185.

141. RICHTER, JURIUS, Evangelische Missionskunde. – Auseinandersetzung des Christentums mit den nichtchristlichen Religionen. Leipzig, 1920, 463 pp.

142. ROCHEDIEU, EDMOND, La Pensée Occidentale face à la Sagesse de l'Orient. In: Asiatische Studien 1954, pp. 1–4; 20–27.

143. RONCAGLIA, MARTINIANO, Oriente e Occidente. I compiti odierui dei missionari in Oriente e il problema della collaborazione e dell' adattamento. In: Neue Zeitschrift für Missionswissenschaft 1954, pp. 1–8; 123–133.

144. ROSENKRANZ, GERHARD, Der Geist Europas und die Religionen des Ostens. In: Zeitschrift fuer Theologie und Kirche 1950, pp. 104–144.

145. ROSENKRANZ, GERHARD, Evangelische Religionskunde – Einführung in eine theologische Schau der Religionen. Tübingen, 1951, 258 pp.

146. ROSS, FLOYD HIAT, Addressed to Christians – Isolationism vs. World Community. New York 1950, 154 pp.

147. ROSS, FLOYD HIAT, A Re-Examination of Christian Attitudes towards other Faiths. In: The Journal of Bible and Religion 1953, pp. 79–83.

148. ROSS, FLOYD HIAT & HILLS, T. W., Questions that Matther most asked by the World Religions. New York, 1954, 266 pp.

149. ROTH, CECIL, The Jewish Contribution to Civilization, London 1938.

150. ROTH, LEON, Jewish Thought as a Factor in Civilization. UNESCO, Paris, 1954, 64 pp.

151. SARKISYANZ, EMANUEL, Russland und der Messianismus des Orients. Sendungsbewusstsein und politischer Chiliasmus des Ostens. Tübingen, 1955, 419 pp.

152. SAUNDERS, KENNETH JAMES, The Ideals of East and West. Cambridge, 1934, 248 pp.

153. SCHECHTER, SOLOMON, Aspects of Rabbinic Theology, New York, 1909, Ch. XIII.

154. SCHECHTER, SOLOMON, Studies in Judaism, Philadelphia, 1896 etc. (3 vols).

155. SCHLUNK, MARTIN, Die Weltreligionen und das Christentum – eine Auseinandersetzung vom Christentum aus. 1932. Revised Editn, Frankfurt/M, 1953, 200 pp.

156. SCHOLEM, G. G., Major Trends in Jewish Mysticism, Jerusalem 1941.

157. SCHOMERUS, HILKO WIARDO, Das Geistesleben der nicht-christlichen Voelker und das Christentum – eine Aufforderung zur Auseinandersetzung der beiden Groessen miteinander, Leipzig, 1914, 95 pp.

158. SCHOMERUS, HILKO WIARDO, Indische Erloesungslehren. Ihre Bedeutung fuer das Verständniss des Christentums. Gütersloh, 1919, 232 pp.

159. SCHMIDT, WILHELM, Die Volker in der Heilsgeschichte der Menschheit. Kaldenkirchen, 1953, 62 pp.

160. SCHUON, FRITHJOF, The Transcendent Unity of Religions. London and New York, 1953, 199 pp.

161. SCHUSTER, HERMANN, Der Christliche Glaube und die Religionen der Völker. Frankfurt/M 1951, 54 pp.

162. SCHWARTZ, LEO, (ed) Great Ages and Ideas of the Jewish People, New York 1956.

163. SHEBBEARE, CHARLES JOHN, Christianity and other Religions. London, 1939, 151 pp.

164. SILVER, ABBA HILLEL, Where Judaism Differed. New York 1956, 318 pp.

165. SIMON, GOTTFRIED, Die Auseinandersetzung des Christentums mit der ausser-christlichen Mystik. Gütersloh, 1931, 110 pp.
166. SIMON, GOTTFRIED, Die Welt des Islam und ihre Beziehungen mit der Christenheit. Gütersloh, 1948, 693 pp.
167. SÖDERBLOM, NATHAN, Der lebendige Gott im Zeugnis der Religionsgeschichte. Gifford Lectures. Edited by Friedrich Heiler, München, 1942, 385 pp.
168. SOPER, EDMUND DAVISON, The Inevitable Choice – Vedanta Philosophy or Christian Gospel. London, 1957, 196 pp.
169. SPIEGELBERG, FRIEDRICH H., Die Profanisierung des japanischen Geistes, als religionsgeschichtliches Phänomen dargestellt an Hand einer Analyse der Farben-holzschnitte des "Ukiyo-e". Leipzig, 1929.
170. STEINBERG, MILTON, Basic Judaism, New York 1947.
171. STEWART, J. LEIGHTON, Chinese Culture and Christianity – a review of China's religious and related systems from the Christian standpoint. New York and London, 1926, 316 pp.
172. SUNDAR SINGH, SADHU, The Search after Reality – Thoughts on Hinduism, Buddhism, Mohammedanism and Christianity. London, 1923, 104 pp.
173. SUZUKI, DAISETZU, Mysticism: Christian and Buddhist. New York, 1957, 214 pp.
174. SUZUKI, DAISETZU, Zen Buddhism, New York 1956, 294 pp.
175. TISDALL, W. CLAIR, Christianity and other Faiths – an essay in comparative religion. London 1912, 252 pp.
176. TOYNBEE, ARNOLD J., Islam and Ourselves. In: Atlantic Monthly 1930, pp. 114–21.
177. UNDERWOOD, A. C., Conversion, Christian and non-Christian. A comparative psychological study. London, 1925, 283 pp.
178. UNESCO. Humanisme et Education en Orient et en Occident – Entretien inter-national, organisé par l'Unesco. Unité et diversité culturelles. Paris, 1953.
179. VICEDOM, GEORG, Die Weltreligionen im Angriff auf die Christenheit. München, 1956, 32 pp.
180. VOSS, CARL HERMANN, The Universal God, the eternal quest in which all men are brothers. New York, 1953, 306 pp.
181. WACH, JOACHIM, General Revelation and the Religions of the World. In: Journal of Bible and Religion, 1954, 83 pp.
182. WACH, JOACHIM, Types of Religious Experience. Christian and non-Christian. Chicago, 1951, 275 pp.
183. WARNECK, GUSTAV, Missionsmotiv und Missionsaufgabe nach der modernen Religionsgeschichtlichen Schule. Berlin, 1907, 45 pp.
184. WATTS, ALAN W., The Supreme Identity, a study of eastern thought in relation to the Christian religion. London 1950, 204 pp.
185. WAXMAN, MEYER, A History of Jewish Literature, New York, 1930–1941.
186. WEI, FRANCIS CHO-MIN, Spirit of Chinese Culture. New York 1947, 186 pp.
187. WEINRICH, FRIEDRICH, Die Liebe im Buddhismus und im Christentum. Berlin, 1935, 115 pp.
188. WHITE, WILLIAM CHARLES, Chinese Jews. 3 vols. Toronto 1942.
189. WIELENGA, D. K., Is het Christendom Relatief of Absoluut Onderscheiden van de Niet-Christelijke Religie? In: De Macedoniër 1927, pp. 193–203.
190. WINSLOW, J. C., The Indian Mystic – some thoughts on India's contribution to Christianity. London, 1926, 71 pp.
191. WITTE, JOHANNES, Das Christentum und die andern Religionen der Erde. In: Neue Allgemeine Missionszeitschrift 1930, pp. 33–39; 78–87; 119–126.
192. WITTE, JOHANNES, Die Christusbotschaft und die Religionen. Gottingen, 1936, 279 pp.
193. WITTE, JOHANNES, Japan zwischen zwei Kulturen. Leipzig, 1928, 505 pp.

194. WITTE, JOHANNES, Zur Propaganda des japanischen Buddhismus in China und zur Propaganda der Religionen überhaupt. In: Christliche Welt 1915, p. 34.
195. WOLFF, OTTO, Indien-Christentum-Abendland. Berlin, 1953, 101 pp.
196. WOLFSON, HARRY AUSTRYN, Philo; Foundation of Religious Philosophy in Judaism, Christianity and Islam. Cambridge, 1948.
197. WU, JOHN C. H., Beyond East and West. New York, 1951, 364 pp.
198. WÜNSCH, GEORG, Das völkische Verständnis der Weltreligionen und die Absolutheit des Christentums. Berlin 1940, 79 pp.
199. YOUNG, CUYLER (ed), Near East Culture and Society. A symposium on the meeting of East and West. Princeton 1951, London 1952.

ADDENDUM

References on Recent Protestant Reports

1. *The Jerusalem Meeting of the International Missionary Council.* March 24–April 8, 1928 (International Missionary Council, New York–London). Pages 404–405 of Volume I, "The Christian Life and Message in Relation to Non-Christian Systems of Thought and Life."
2. *The Christian Message in a Non-Christian World*, by Hendrik Kraemer, Harper and Brothers, 1939. Reprint, 1958 (Kregel Publications).
3. *The World Mission of the Church* – Findings and Recommendations of the International Missionary Council, Tambaram, Madras, India, December 12–29, 1938. (International Missionary Council, London).
4. *The Authority of the Faith* (Volume I of "The Madras Series"). (International Missionary Council, New York–London, 1939). Pages 1–5.
5. *Renewal and Advance* – "Christian Witness in a Revolutionary World." Edited by C. W. Ranson (Pages 212–213). (International Missionary Council, London–Edinburgh House Press, 1948).
6. *Missions Under the Cross* – Edited by Norman Goodall (The addresses, statements and reports from the meeting of the International Missionary Council, Willingen, Germany, July 1952). Page 190.
7. *The Evanston Report* – Edited by W. A. Visser 't Hooft. The Second Assembly of the World Council of Churches, 1954 (Harper). Page 100.
8. *The Evanston Report* – Pages 106–107.